Teaching Undergraduate Research in Religious Studies

AMERICAN ACADEMY OF RELIGION

TEACHING RELIGIOUS STUDIES SERIES

SERIES EDITOR
Susan Henking
Hobart and William Smith Colleges

A Publication Series of
The American Academy of Religion
and
Oxford University Press

TEACHING LEVI-STRAUSS
Edited by Hans H. Penner

TEACHING ISLAM
Edited by Brannon M. Wheeler

TEACHING FREUD
Edited by Diane Jonte-Pace

TEACHING DURKHEIM
Edited by Terry F. Godlove, Jr.

TEACHING AFRICAN AMERICAN RELIGIONS
Edited by Carolyn M. Jones and Theodore Louis Trost

TEACHING RELIGION AND HEALING
Edited by Linda L. Barnes and Inés Talamantez

TEACHING NEW RELIGIOUS MOVEMENTS
Edited by David G. Bromley

TEACHING RITUAL
Edited by Catherine Bell

TEACHING CONFUCIANISM
Jeffrey L. Richey

TEACHING THE DAODE JING
Edited by Gary Delaney DeAngelis and Warren G. Frisina

TEACHING RELIGION AND FILM
Gregory J. Watkins

TEACHING DEATH AND DYING
Edited by Christopher M. Moreman

TEACHING UNDERGRADUATE RESEARCH IN RELIGIOUS STUDIES
Edited by Bernadette McNary-Zak and Rebecca Todd Peters

Teaching Undergraduate Research in Religious Studies

EDITED BY
BERNADETTE MCNARY-ZAK
AND REBECCA TODD PETERS

OXFORD
UNIVERSITY PRESS

OXFORD
UNIVERSITY PRESS

Oxford University Press, Inc., publishes works that further
Oxford University's objective of excellence
in research, scholarship, and education.

Oxford   New York
Auckland   Cape Town   Dar es Salaam   Hong Kong   Karachi
Kuala Lumpur   Madrid   Melbourne   Mexico City   Nairobi
New Delhi   Shanghai   Taipei   Toronto

With offices in
Argentina   Austria   Brazil   Chile   Czech Republic   France   Greece
Guatemala   Hungary   Italy   Japan   Poland   Portugal   Singapore
South Korea   Switzerland   Thailand   Turkey   Ukraine   Vietnam

Copyright © 2011 by Oxford University Press, Inc.

Published by Oxford University Press, Inc.
198 Madison Avenue, New York, New York 10016

www.oup.com

Oxford is a registered trademark of Oxford University Press

Library of Congress Cataloging-in-Publication Data

Teaching undergraduate research in religious studies/edited by
Bernadette McNary-Zak and Rebecca Todd Peters.
    p.   cm.
Includes bibliographical references and index.
ISBN 978-0-19-973286-9
1. Religion—Methodology.   2. Religion—Study and teaching.   I. McNary-Zak, Bernadette.
II. Peters, Rebecca Todd.   III. Title.
BL41.T455 2011
200.71'1—dc22   2010049026

9 8 7 6 5 4 3 2 1

Printed in the United States of America
on acid-free paper

Acknowledgments

The essays in this volume emerge from sustained discussion about the
ways Undergraduate Research might best serve teachers and students in
Religious Studies. They are the product of considerable collaboration
and conversation from 2007 to 2009. We are grateful to so many for
their contribution to this effort. Several institutions provided financial
support for our work. Special thanks go to the Wabash Center for
Teaching and Learning in Theology and Religion and to several
cosponsoring institutions including Elon University, Lafayette College,
Lenoir-Rhyne University, St. Olaf College, and Texas Christian
University. We are also grateful for the hospitality of Elon University
president, Leo Lambert, and of the members of the Department of
Religious Studies at Elon during two weekend meetings over the course
of our work. We gathered in April 2007 as a Consultation of sixteen
faculty members from various institutions across the country to share
current practices in Undergraduate Research and to discuss common
standards. In September 2007, thirteen members from the
Consultation formed a Working Group to focus our conversations on
some of the features of Undergraduate Research as a distinctive pedagogy. The members of the Working Group were Jeffrey M. Brackett,
Mark Gstohl, Lynn R. Huber, Nadia Lahutsky, John R. Lanci, Bernadette
McNary-Zak, Carolyn M. Jones, Paul O. Myhre, Maggie Odell, Rebecca
Todd Peters, David C. Ratke, Robin Rinehart, and Steve Stell; the three
additional members of the original Consultation were Marcia Bunge,
Jim Linville, and Bella Mukonyora. The Working Statement on

Undergraduate Research in Religious Studies (found in Appendix I) is a product of the work of these two groups.

Opportunities to present portions of our work at meetings of the American Academy of Religion and the Council of Undergraduate Research helped us refine our thinking about the distinctiveness of this pedagogy in humanities disciplines. Special thanks to Tim Renick for inviting us to present some of our work at a 2007 AAR Leadership Workshop titled "The Religion Major and Liberal Education."

Bonnie Bruno and Lorraine Allen at Elon University and Rita Arthur at the Wabash Center for Teaching and Learning in Theology and Religion provided help with reporting. We also wish to thank Beth De Ford, Peter Felten, Lucinda Huffaker, Paul Miller, Dena Pence, Jeffrey Pugh, Emily Shore, Robert Strandburg, and Karl Sienerth for their material support and abiding interest in improving pedagogy and Undergraduate Research in our discipline; Brandon Cornett, Elizabeth Dunnam, Nevada Drollinger, Lindsey Hammond, Erin Keys, Shelton Oakley, and Daniel Webb, former students who offered reflections on their Undergraduate Research experiences; and the Hatcher Peters family: Jeff, Sophie, Eve, and Becky; and the Zak family: David, Elizabeth, and David Michael; for their support and encouragement.

Our final and deepest thanks are to our students. They remain our richest conversation partners. This book is dedicated to them.

Contents

Contributors

Jeffrey M. Brackett is Associate Professor of Religious Studies at Ball State University, Muncie, Indiana. He was the recipient of a Fulbright-Hays Dissertation Research Grant, among others, for research on contemporary Hinduism. He writes about Hinduism, teaching religion, and ethnography.

Ann Marie Leonard Chilton is an Adjunct English Instructor at Forsyth Technical Community College in Winston-Salem, North Carolina. She has a B.A. in Religious Studies and English from Elon University and an M.F.A. in Creative Nonfiction from Queens University of Charlotte.

Mark Gstohl is Associate Professor of Theology at Xavier University of Louisiana, where he also serves as the Faculty-in-Residence for Service-Learning in the Center for the Advancement of Teaching. He teaches historical theology and comparative religion. He has written several articles and published *Southern Baptist Theologians and Original Sin* (2004).

Lynn R. Huber is Associate Professor of Religious Studies at Elon University in Elon, North Carolina, where she teaches courses on New Testament and early Christianity. She has also published on topics related to teaching the Bible using the visual arts.

Carolyn M. Jones is Associate Professor of Religion and in the Institute for African American Studies at the University of Georgia in Athens. Her areas of specialization are religion and literature with a concentration on African and African American women's writing and religion and theory. She is the coeditor of *Teaching African American Religions* (2005) with Theodore Trost and the author of numerous articles.

Nadia M. Lahutsky is Department Chair and Associate Professor of Religion at Texas Christian University in Fort Worth. A historian of modern Roman Catholicism, she is working on a project investigating Disciples of Christ who were ecumenical observers at Vatican II.

John R. Lanci is Professor of Religious Studies at Stonehill College in Easton, Massachusetts. The author of two books on the New Testament and Christian origins, as well as a number of articles on teaching religion, he was the recipient of Stonehill's Hegarty Award for Excellence in Teaching in 1996 and currently serves as the inaugural faculty fellow in the college's Center for Teaching and Learning.

Bernadette McNary-Zak is Associate Professor of Religious Studies at Rhodes College in Memphis, Tennessee. She is a historian of early Christianity with a particular focus on Christian monasticism. Her current book project examines contemporary Roman Catholic interpretations of ancient desert eremitic practices.

Paul O. Myhre is Associate Director for the Wabash Center for Teaching and Learning in Theology and Religion. He has recently published *Introduction to Religious Studies* (2009). His current research and scholarly work involves intersections between art and religion, Mississippian and Adena-Hopewell environmental ethics and religious practice, and religion and ethics in North America. His current book project examines twenty-first century North American issues in relation to religion and ethics.

Rebecca Todd Peters is Department Chair and Associate Professor of Religious Studies at Elon University. She is a Christian social ethicist working primarily on environmental, economic, and globalization ethics. Her current project on solidarity ethics is a follow-up to her book *In Search of the Good Life: The Ethics of Globalization* (2004).

David C. Ratke is Professor of Religious Studies at Lenoir-Rhyne University in Hickory, North Carolina, where he is also the Honors Director. He has written numerous articles and book reviews in Christian theology and is the author of *Confession and Mission, Word and Sacrament* (2001).

Robin Rinehart is Professor of Religious Studies at Lafayette College. She received the Lindback Foundation Award for distinguished teaching in 2010. Her books include *Contemporary Hinduism* (2004) and *Debating the Dasam Granth* (2011).

Teaching Undergraduate Research in Religious Studies

I

Theorizing Undergraduate Research in Religious Studies

Bernadette McNary-Zak and Rebecca Todd Peters

In the fall of 2001 we both began our first tenure-track positions in religious studies departments at church-related liberal arts institutions. By our second year, we had each been asked to mentor undergraduate students in projects that fell under the institutional rubric of "Undergraduate Research."[1] While we had each written advanced theses during our own undergraduate days that are parallel to what is now being called "Undergraduate Research," this nomenclature and the accompanying trend in higher education to promote intensive, individualized opportunities for substantive and original research at the undergraduate level has increased markedly in the humanities in the last ten years. While we each enthusiastically embraced the possibility for mentoring students, this was quickly tempered by the realization that there were few resources in the humanities to support our efforts.

We share an approach to pedagogy that recognizes good teaching as a process of figuring out how to connect ideas, materials, and concepts with varied groups of students day in and day out. Consequently, we believe that innovation, improvisation, and spontaneity are necessary hallmarks of good teaching. Through experimentation, trial, and error we learned that some kinds of research projects and experiences were successful while others were not, and our conversations with our peers yielded similar stories. We also recognized that while our ability to innovate and respond to student requests for new forms of engaged learning in the form of

Undergraduate Research was a reasonable expectation on the part of our students and our institutions, it was neither efficient nor effective to expect individual faculty members across the country to reinvent the wheel.

As we discussed our own best practices and compared our definitions of what we regarded as sufficient quality for student work in Undergraduate Research with each other and with colleagues, we recognized that we were mentoring student projects in many different ways with different degrees of success. Through these informal conversations we recognized that student work yielded varying results and levels of quality in the finished project. Increased involvement with mentoring students and attention to the national conversations about Undergraduate Research in higher education convinced us that there would be an increasing demand for religious studies faculty to participate in mentoring Undergraduate Research. Our interest in establishing rigorous standards for this new pedagogy in the field of religious studies prompted us to initiate a broader conversation in the field about the need for disciplinary standards of excellence that would help define what it is we expect when undergraduate students engage in the practice of Undergraduate Research in our discipline.

Background for Undergraduate Research

The first task to address as we move forward in thinking about Undergraduate Research is defining our terms. If it seems obvious to us that all students are engaged in research and writing at some level in their undergraduate work, then what exactly do we mean by the use of the term *Undergraduate Research*? Indeed, undergraduate students engage in multiple forms of research activities as a part of fulfilling general education and departmental requirements. These research experiences include but are not limited to preliminary work in introductory and research methods courses as well as more advanced research papers in upper-level courses, capstones, or senior seminars.

We intend Undergraduate Research as a technical term that does not refer to all research done by undergraduate students. Undergraduate Research is distinct from other research requirements as it entails a more intensive and extensive research experience than traditional forms of research with students in the discipline. Drawing on the classroom experience of designing research and writing papers, Undergraduate Research explores a focused, discrete body of knowledge in preparation for developing a research question, a research agenda, and a research product. As a result, Undergraduate Research often assumes the form of an independent study, honors research, tutorial, or summer research fellow.

The purpose of Undergraduate Research is to move beyond the typical expectations of departmental course work by striving to train students who have the capacity and desire to envision, sustain, and complete a complex, high-quality, and nuanced analysis in the methodological and research tools of the discipline; to prepare them for continued study in the field; and to foster independent, intellectual development. This is consonant with the Council on Undergraduate Research's (CUR) definition of Undergraduate Research as "an inquiry or investigation conducted by an undergraduate student that makes an original intellectual or creative contribution to the discipline."[2]

The institutionalization of Undergraduate Research as a distinct pedagogy within higher education originated in the field of chemistry as a way to promote independent thinking and original research among undergraduates through an apprenticeship model of education. In 1978, a group of chemists formed CUR as a national organization to support and promote this pedagogy in chemistry programs at private liberal arts colleges.[3] Gradually, the organization expanded to include the disciplines of biology, geosciences, mathematics and computer science, physics and astronomy, psychology, and the social sciences.

The fact that the institutionalization of Undergraduate Research originated in the natural sciences is not surprising given the collaborative approach to scholarship that characterizes research in the natural sciences. The nature of lab work facilitates the incorporation of research students in ways that are often incompatible with research in humanities. When the traditional model of Undergraduate Research is predicated on incorporating undergraduate students into a faculty member's research project, the very nature of work in the humanities often makes it difficult for humanities scholars to imagine how to go about mentoring students in Undergraduate Research.

Currently, institutions across the country are encouraging and supporting faculty in all disciplines to incorporate this pedagogy into their departmental programs. The impact of the educational reforms of the 1980s and 1990s continue to give grounding to their efforts. In her work on the impact of The Boyer Commission, Wendy Katkin observes that the commission's 1998 report "was driven by the conviction that research universities are uniquely positioned to offer an undergraduate education that takes advantage of the immense resources of their research and graduate programs and that makes 'research-based learning the standard.'"[4] In addition to institutional and national emphases on expanding Undergraduate Research opportunities for students across the country, increasing numbers of faculty are recognizing the value of working with undergraduate students in intensive mentoring relationships for improving their own teaching as well as improving student learning (see chapter 3 for a more detailed discussion).

In 2008, the members of CUR voted to create a new division dedicated to those disciplines in the arts and humanities. While Undergraduate Research has certainly been taking place in a variety of forms in the arts and humanities, it has, for the most part, lacked a formal or centralized forum for resources, funding, and sharing ideas and practices. As a result, the decision by CUR to expand representation marks a potentially significant moment of promise in the development of Undergraduate Research as professors in these disciplines determine how to articulate their role in the national conversation and effect the continuing growth of this pedagogy.

Religious studies faculty who are engaged in mentoring Undergraduate Research recognize several significant benefits for students who pursue the types of focused, intensive research projects that fall within the rubric of Undergraduate Research. These benefits include richer engagement with a focused content area; honing critical thinking, research, writing and presentation skills; and building competence and confidence (see chapter 10 for further discussion). Psychology professor, David Lopatto, has argued that Undergraduate Research helps to "realize the goals of liberal education" because it fosters personal growth and development as well as providing professional skills for students.[5] These benefits are also identified by students. In a study that examined the summer Undergraduate Research programs of four liberal arts colleges recognized for excellence in Undergraduate Research, Lopatto found that science, social science, and humanities students all rated the benefits of "learning a topic in depth," "developing a continuing relationship with a faculty member," "understanding the research process in your field," and "readiness for more demanding research" very highly.[6] While the research process will necessarily differ among the natural sciences, social sciences, and the humanities, these findings highlight that there are significant similarities in the value of Undergraduate Research to student development that occur across all three modes of inquiry. Given the recent increase in Undergraduate Research in the humanities, further research on its effectiveness needs to be undertaken.

Offering Criteria for Undergraduate Research in Religious Studies

Precisely because the practice of Undergraduate Research in religious studies is such a recent phenomenon, there are not yet standards in our discipline that define what counts as Undergraduate Research and benchmark what qualifies as excellence. In order to begin to address these deficiencies, we formed a Working Group of thirteen scholars of religious studies representing a range of subdisciplinary and institutional contexts that gathered several times over a three-year period to give sustained attention to Undergraduate Research in our discipline. The criteria offered here were generated by the Working Group (see Appendix I: Working Statement on Undergraduate Research in Religious Studies).

Learning goals are certainly an important aspect of any pedagogical approach. As faculty and students work together to map these learning goals, they should pay particular attention to what can and ought to be learned in an Undergraduate Research project. When we considered the contributions that Undergraduate Research can make to the learning process of undergraduate students in religious studies departments, we identified several basic learning goals as important aspects of this pedagogy. Undergraduate Research should be framed around the cultivation of independent thinking and developing one's voice and contribution. Seeing familiar and odd conjunctions between topics should reinforce learning and contribute to new frames of understanding. As a form of research, Undergraduate Research requires students to ask questions, conduct investigations, and build methodological skills in systematic ways; it is also incumbent on the student to seek theories, answers, or solutions. In this way, Undergraduate Research is a form of training the student to identify gathered knowledge in a way typical of an experienced practitioner or expert in the discipline, and to share that knowledge in public forums.

Learning Goals of Undergraduate Research in Religious Studies

- to cultivate independent thinking.
- to cultivate an academic voice.
- to develop an original contribution.
- to see familiar and odd conjunctions between topics that could both reinforce learning and contribute to explorations into new frames of understanding.
- to demonstrate capacity for communication of research discoveries through presentations and papers.
- to seek their own theories, answers, or solutions.
- to conduct investigations, building methodological skills in systematic ways.
- to identify gathered knowledge in a way typical of an experienced practitioner.

In our efforts to theorize the foundations of Undergraduate Research in religious studies we identified four criteria that define this pedagogy as distinct from other forms of research in a typical program of study in the discipline. Given that these criteria remain contested within our own Working Group, we offer them in this venue to prompt discussion, dialogue, and debate with our colleagues in the discipline about the role and function of Undergraduate Research in departments of religious studies across the country.

Original Intellectual or Creative Contribution to the Discipline

Our Working Group focused its initial efforts on the question of whether the CUR definition can and should apply to Undergraduate Research in our discipline. While we readily agreed with the first part of the CUR definition that Undergraduate Research constitutes "an inquiry or investigation conducted by an undergraduate student," we were not in agreement about whether or not it was necessary or even possible for undergraduates to make an "original intellectual or creative contribution to the discipline." We asked directly and specifically whether, and how, categories of "original" and "contribution" were defined in the field and, from there, whether they were categories that we could, or should, apply to Undergraduate Research. Given that these were categories defined by and through the experience of Undergraduate Research in the natural sciences, we wondered whether or not they were adequate for the purposes and intentions of Undergraduate Research in religious studies. We were hard pressed to replace these categories outright with more appropriate ones because we had not yet acquired a sufficiently clear understanding of how we envisioned the research process and product of Undergraduate Research. As we probed the boundaries and guidelines for conducting Undergraduate Research in the various fields of religious studies, we recognized that our interpretation and application of the categories of "original" and "contribution" would necessarily have to be broad enough to incorporate the multiplicity of methods and approaches, as well as the distinctive models of inquiry, that are extant in our discipline. Moreover, we also acknowledged that the ways in which we understand "original intellectual or creative contribution" will vary depending on the specific project at hand and that this is a reflection of the epistemological variety in the humanities (see chapter 2 for a more detailed discussion).

In an effort to recast the CUR definition in a way that is appropriate for the discipline of religious studies, we interpreted "original intellectual or creative contribution" to include encountering/uncovering new data which are incorporated into existing frameworks, discovering new insights or new data that alter the boundaries and/or contours of the field, drawing novel comparisons or making heretofore unrecognized connections within the field, making new assessments of current knowledge/interpretations based on such standards, creating new visions or interpretive structures that re-integrate/ reconfigure what is already known or accepted, applying existing interpretive structures in a new way or in new contexts in order to unfold distinctive integrations/configurations within the field.[7] Some approaches that produce original and creative work within Undergraduate Research in religious studies include the following: archival; ethnographic; textual studies; historical studies; cultural studies (see chapters 5, 6, 7, 8, and 9 for examples of these approaches). The multidisciplinary character of religious studies means "original" or "creative" contributions will vary depending on the specific project at hand.

An original intellectual or creative contribution in Undergraduate Research in Religious Studies includes:

- encountering/uncovering new data which are incorporated into existing frameworks
- discovering new insights or new data that alter the boundaries and/or contours of the field
- drawing novel comparisons or making heretofore unrecognized connections within the field
- making new assessments of current knowledge/interpretations based on such standards
- creating new visions or interpretive structures that re-integrate/ reconfigure what is already known or accepted
- applying existing interpretive structures in a new way or in new contexts in order to unfold distinctive integrations/configurations within the field

---

Selective

Undergraduate Research builds on the acquisition of prior skills as well as the student's broader knowledge base. Undergraduate Research requires students to critically examine an area of deep interest in the discipline in a more complex and nuanced manner then regular course requirements allow. Although it is a defining feature of this pedagogy, selectivity should not mean that Undergraduate Research is restricted to the best and brightest students but, rather, that it is intended for those students with a certain curiosity and capability. While Undergraduate Research may assume some familiarity with content material in a particular area, and a capacity for working with research methods, the emphasis is on having an ability to ask questions and investigate issues in ways representative of the discipline. One of the characteristics that makes Undergraduate Research unique from other forms of research done by undergraduates is that this introduction to the discipline and disciplinary modes of inquiry occurs through individualized attention provided by a professor to a student project. Furthermore, the depth and breadth of work that a student puts into an Undergraduate Research project form a unique student-faculty interaction. The fact that faculty are only able to individually mentor a select number of students also contributes to the selectivity of Undergraduate Research.

Collaborative

Undergraduate Research is a collaborative enterprise, as both faculty and student(s) work together to contribute to the research project. This collaborative effort represents a unique relationship between faculty and student(s), in which both parties contribute to the research agenda and the final product. While Undergraduate Research can build on knowledge and skills gained in the research assistant model, the collaborative requirement of Undergraduate Research means that it must go beyond this model to create distinctive work that allows for a significant scholarly contribution by the student. Attention to the diversity of our experiences with Undergraduate Research led us to map the extent and forms of collaboration in Undergraduate Research as a continuum where, at one end, faculty assign a topic and together with the student(s) cooperate in developing the research process and, at the other end, faculty and student(s) are in a collegial relationship in which they work together on a common research project resulting in a coauthored final product.

Public

One final criterion of Undergraduate Research that distinguishes it from more common forms of research expected of undergraduates is its public nature. Undergraduate Research is public insofar as it is of such quality that its public dissemination is warranted and expected. Public dissemination can assume a variety of forms ranging from a public presentation on a student's own campus to journal publication or conference presentation. In all cases, public dissemination requires the student to engage with others outside the mentoring relationship about the research process and product. As a result, it models scholarly activity in the discipline and provides both an essential and necessary means of assessment and evaluation of Undergraduate Research.

Prevailing Questions for Religious Studies

The essays in this volume address the theoretical and practical dimensions of Undergraduate Research in religious studies. This book has been designed so that the chapters may be read individually or in sequence, depending on the specific areas of interest to the reader. For those new to Undergraduate Research, this book provides an overview of fundamental issues and pedagogical questions that relate to the practice of Undergraduate Research in religious studies and practical models for application in the classroom. For seasoned mentors of Undergraduate Research in the discipline, this book serves as a dialogue partner on emerging issues and insight into pertinent questions in the discipline. While we have attempted to demonstrate the ways in which Undergraduate Research is distinct from other undergraduate experiences of research, many of the issues and topics addressed by the authors of this book are transferable to a variety of pedagogical settings in which students are required to do other forms of research.

In many ways, the authors of these essays represent the face of religious studies departments across the country, composed of persons in distinct fields, each with highly specific methodological training, and contributing to the commonly constructed subject of the academic study of religion. We represent a variety of institutions, ranging from small liberal arts colleges to research universities, from religiously affiliated colleges to historically black universities. Our social locations range from smaller cities in Minnesota, Pennsylvania, and North Carolina to urban centers in Texas, Louisiana, Georgia, and Tennessee.

The essays in this book are intended to offer three contributions to the development of Undergraduate Research in the discipline of religious studies. In the first section of the book, contributors frame a number of the theoretical and epistemological issues that are particular to thinking about Undergraduate Research in the humanities, and even more specifically in religious studies. These essays are intended to prompt discussion, dialogue, and debate about serious issues related to the development of Undergraduate Research within our discipline. Such collegial interaction is necessary if we are to develop standards of rigor and respectability within our field regarding the value and expectations of high-quality Undergraduate Research. In the second section of the book, experienced teachers and mentors offer their insights and reflections on creating excellence in Undergraduate Research using five distinct methodologies. The use of their own experiences and student work reveals a pedagogical grounding that can serve as a model for faculty interested in pursuing Undergraduate Research with their own student body. The final section of the book is focused on discussing practical tools and advice for engaging in Undergraduate Research and improving the quality and support of Undergraduate Research in religious studies. The book ends with an Afterword by a former student who discusses the importance that Undergraduate Research played in her development as a young person, a student, and a scholar. Additionally, interspersed throughout the text, there are quotes from former students reflecting on their experiences of Undergraduate Research.

While the past three years have afforded significant progress for our Working Group to develop the conversation about the role and function of Undergraduate Research in religious studies, it is also important to begin to articulate potential challenges and obstacles to supporting Undergraduate Research in religious studies that the American Academy of Religion, the Society of Biblical Literature, and colleagues of other professional societies may need to address in the coming years. We will conclude this essay by highlighting some concerns that warrant further discussion and attention.

Science Model

As we have already indicated, for many years Undergraduate Research has primarily been associated with the natural sciences. The traditional science model that shaped the development of Undergraduate Research is rooted in mentoring students into one's discipline by incorporating them into a scholar's existing research agenda. Laboratory science lends itself to a collaborative approach to scholarship and facilitates the incorporation of research students in ways that are more difficult in the humanities. Since research in the humanities has traditionally been a solitary effort and publications are primarily single-authored, the model of scholarly collaboration has not been the norm. The necessity of ancient and modern languages in many subdisciplines within religious studies adds to the difficulty of incorporating students into existing research projects. Additionally the normative and constructive character of much work in theology and ethics often requires broader and deeper knowledge in the field than most undergraduates are able to acquire. Many of these factors have contributed to a historic paucity of Undergraduate Research within the field of religious studies. While many of the essays in this book address these challenges and begin to reframe how we approach the task of Undergraduate Research from the perspective of our field, we anticipate that the dominance of the "science model" of Undergraduate

Research will continue to impact the conversations about Undergraduate Research in religious studies in years to come. Additionally, the potential contributions that religious studies faculty stand to make to the larger conversations about Undergraduate Research within the Council on Undergraduate Research and other professional venues have the possibility of challenging the dominance of the natural sciences model and helping reframe common assumptions and expectations about Undergraduate Research more broadly.

Resistance from Religious Studies Faculty

Another significant factor in promoting Undergraduate Research in religious studies is resistance from some colleagues in the field. Largely because most academics associate Undergraduate Research with the scientific and laboratory model, faculty often assume that mentoring Undergraduate Research will require them to incorporate students into their own research projects. Many faculty are justifiably reluctant to revise or shape their research agenda in ways that facilitate student participation. However, this resistance is more a reflection of the limitations of the scientific model of Undergraduate Research as a functional and productive model for religious studies, than a problematic aspect of Undergraduate Research as an effective pedagogy in the field of religious studies. As this volume demonstrates, there are a wide variety of approaches to take as we think about how to mentor students and how to guide effective and meaningful research projects for undergraduate students. While some faculty only agree to mentor projects that fall within the boundaries of their own research agenda (which is quite different from incorporating them into one's own research project), others are willing to mentor students in a broader range of topics. Certainly further discussions about the role of mentoring and the content of student projects are important as we proceed, but overcoming resistance from our colleagues will likely be furthered through the development of models for Undergraduate Research that are more authentic to our field.

Reward and Tenure Systems

Institutional barriers are another hurdle that we face in promoting interest in Undergraduate Research given the significant demands that are placed on individual faculty members' time. While for some faculty, the mentoring of Undergraduate Research may contribute to and support their own research agenda, we propose that mentoring Undergraduate Research be recognized as falling within our teaching responsibilities as faculty. Intensive mentoring of a single student over several semesters is often difficult for many faculty to entertain when the current pressures on their time from research, teaching, and service expectations are often already overwhelming. Institutions and administrators who value this kind of intensive and formative pedagogy both for individual students and for institutional reputations will have to figure out how to offer institutional compensation either in the form of financial compensation or teaching credit. For faculty in religious studies to be able to participate in mentoring Undergraduate Research, the increased demands of time and energy required to do so effectively must be accompanied by concrete remuneration. We also recognize that faculty who are negotiating tenure and promotion systems will need to have formal institutional assurance that working with Undergraduate Research is recognized as a valued component of their teaching responsibilities.

Other Issues

Other issues that will need to be addressed in the future include generating additional venues for the dissemination of student research. Current venues include the National Conferences for Undergraduate Research, regional American Academy of Religion and Society of Biblical Literature meetings, and the Theta Alpha Kappa journal. There is, as well, a need for ongoing conversation about how to select which students one will mentor. The assumption within Undergraduate Research is that the process can be important for any student, but often resources are diverted for the "best and the brightest" students. Surely, many more issues can and will be identified in the coming years as conversations develop more broadly in our field.

Interest in Undergraduate Research appears to be increasing across the country and many faculty who teach religious studies in primarily undergraduate institutions can expect to see an increase in institutional expectations and pressure to participate in emerging and developing programs of Undergraduate Research. The 2002 report from the Association of American Colleges and Universities, *Greater Expectations: A New Vision for Learning as a Nation Goes to College*, promotes increasing Undergraduate Research opportunities.[8] While some faculty may shy away from participating in Undergraduate Research because it smacks of the latest "fad" in higher education, if appropriate institutional support for Undergraduate Research is put in place, the intellectual and professional rewards for students, faculty, and institutions make participating in this growing movement worthwhile. Our hope for Undergraduate Research in religious studies in ten years is to see strong institutional and guild support for faculty mentoring of Undergraduate Research so that faculty who are interested will be able to participate in Undergraduate Research programs in meaningful and fulfilling ways.

Student Reflections on the Benefits of Undergraduate Research

Erin Keys

I would say that the most pivotal aspect of my college career was participating in Undergraduate Research. The lasting effects of Undergraduate Research more than prepared me for master's-level work in Religious Studies and, in fact, put my ability for critical and original thought on the level of many students I encountered who were already in the Ph.D. process.... Undergraduate Research also made me a more competitive candidate when it came time to apply for graduate school. I was fully confident in my abilities as a scholar and in fact felt better prepared than many of my other friends who had not been fortunate enough to work with a mentor for the majority of their college career. I know it was the work I did in Undergraduate Research that caused me to be accepted into every master's program to which I applied, many with full scholarships. And ultimately, when it came time to make a decision on graduate school, I know that it was Undergraduate Research, and the ways in which it taught me to think for myself, that allowed me the capacity to make a difficult decision with confidence.

NOTES

1. Throughout the text, we capitalize the term "Undergraduate Research" to indicate our use of the term as a formal and clearly defined activity that differs from research that undergraduates do in the course of the regular degreee programs.

2. The Council on Undergraduate Research is the primary organization dedicated to supporting high-quality Undergraduate Research and scholarship. CUR is made up of affiliated colleges, universities, and individuals who work together to promote and support the development of Undergraduate Research in higher education. See http://www.cur.org/about.html. In 1987, the National Conferences on Undergraduate Research (NCUR) was created as a distinct organization responsible, most prominently, for "promoting undergraduate research, scholarship and creative activity in all fields of study by sponsoring an annual conference for students," http://www.ncur.org/aboutNCUR.html. For over two decades, CUR and NCUR have coexisted and have developed in relative autonomy, serving their respective primary constituencies. Each

organization has witnessed considerable change reflecting, in part, the development and growth of the practice of Undergraduate Research across all disciplines. The two organizations are in the process of merging.

3. For a history of CUR and National Conferences on Undergraduate Research, see Gregory Young, "National Conferences on Undergraduate Research: A Look Back as CUR and National Conferences on Undergraduate Research Join Forces", *CUR Quarterly*, 31, no. 1 (Fall 2010): 27–30.

4. See Wendy Katkin, "The Boyer Commission Report and Its Impact on Undergraduate Research," in "Valuing and Supporting Undergraduate Research," ed. Joyce Kinkead, special issue, *New Directions for Teaching and Learning* 93 (Spring 2003): 24. Here Katkin cites Boyer Commission on Educating Undergraduates in the Research University, *Reinventing Undergraduate Education: A Blueprint for America's Research Universities* (Stony Brook, NY: State University of New York, 1998), 15.

5. David Lopatto, "Undergraduate Research as a Catalyst for Liberal Learning," *Peer Review* 8, no. 1 (Winter 2006): 23.

6. Ibid, 24.

7. While this list is in no way intended to be comprehensive, it does offer a starting point for future conversation.

8. Lopatto, 22.

PART I

Defining Undergraduate Research in Religious Studies

There are several theoretical issues at the pedagogical foundation of Undergraduate Research in religious studies. The chapters in this section provide close examination and discussion of three of these issues, namely, the contribution, mentoring, and methodology of Undergraduate Research in our discipline.

The ways in which we construct meaning in our discipline are shaped by our own social locations and the contexts of the study of religion, the classroom, the institution, and the guild. Given this, the Council on Undergraduate Research definition of Undergraduate Research, founded in the sciences, may not apply accurately to disciplines in the humanities such as religious studies, wherein the operating assumption is that knowledge is constructed, and definitions of originality and creativity are shaped by intersecting contextual concerns and impulses. The first chapter in this section, chapter two, examines the challenge of defining what constitutes an "original contribution to the discipline" in Undergraduate Research in religious studies by considering whether there is something distinct about inquiry in the humanities and in religious studies that provides for a variety of models for Undergraduate Research. Incorporating the perspectives of several of the authors in this volume, this chapter supplies a multifaceted response grounded in different ways of thinking about the process and product of Undergraduate Research in the discipline and in one's area of specialization.

Undergraduate Research provides an opportunity for students to develop scholarly collaborative relationships. Often, the central relationship is that of the faculty member and the student. The second chapter in this section, chapter three, takes up mentoring relationships and discusses how they are contextual and reflect the identities—including gender, age, and race—of all participants. The mentoring relationship begins where the student is in terms of her/his skills, course work, capacities, and abilities; over the course of the undergraduate research period, and given the nature of academic research, it may include a particular personal investment on the part of the mentor as she/he addresses the need for support and confidence building. As in all relationships, self-reflective capacities are required of the mentor and mentee. Both parties need to examine their reasons for their place in the mentoring relationship at the beginning and throughout the Undergraduate Research period. How do power dynamics factor into the mentoring relationship? When and how are boundaries established and maintained between students and faculty? Are there stages in the mentoring relationship? What do students and faculty gain through participation in Undergraduate Research? How is it possible for students and faculty to become collaborators and conversation partners? Our role in the mentoring relationship can have a genuine and lasting impact on a student's academic development.

Religious studies is understood here as a polymethodic discipline in which research is constructive and imaginative in approach. In Undergraduate Research, students can demonstrate independent thinking and the capacity for working with research methods and skills. They can learn to negotiate research obstacles and to communicate results effectively. The third chapter in this section, chapter four, discusses the ways in which Undergraduate Research requires that a student be willing: to acquire more familiarity with the content of the discipline; to engage sources widely, critically, and deeply; and to cultivate a capacity to formulate research questions individually, in collaboration with faculty, and with other students. What are the prerequisite skills and content base required for a student to undertake Undergraduate Research? Should Undergraduate Research in religious studies be restricted to those students who have studied method and theory? Is undergraduate research best suited for particular types of students, specific learning styles, or developmental stages? How should undergraduate research be situated and integrated in the context of institutional mission, departmental offerings, and major requirements? Should undergraduate research help prepare students for graduate study in the discipline? The ways in which we envision the intellectual, academic, and personal goals of Undergraduate Research will influence how we engage our students in this pedagogy.

2

Contributing to the Discipline

Rebecca Todd Peters and Bernadette McNary-Zak

Epistemological Considerations

For those engaged in Undergraduate Research in the humanities, the commitment to research and critical inquiry raises questions about the nature of knowledge itself. Where do our ideas come from? Is what we're saying true? Questions concerning the origins, formation, and validation of knowledge impact the interpretation of what constitutes an "original intellectual and creative contribution" in the humanities. The specific location of religious studies within the humanities raises additional issues concerning epistemologies, social locations, and student formation and development for Undergraduate Research in this discipline. The significance of contextual influences upon a student means that one's location within the broader world impacts the questions one raises, the approaches one uses, what one sees as a meaningful research agenda, and the goals and means through which one conducts and evaluates research.

Students engaged in Undergraduate Research in religious studies are able to recognize there are multiple epistemological perspectives from which to study religion. Whether it is situated in the present or in the past, whether it employs the methods of literary criticism, art history, or ethnography, whether it is archival or phenomenological in approach, whether its focus is in biblical studies or comparative theology, Undergraduate Research in religious studies affirms the claim made by Walter H. Capps that the discipline "has no single subject, nor does it sanction any one method of approach. Rather the subject is multiple, and the methods of approach are numerous."[1]

As Undergraduate Research increases in visibility in higher education and becomes a more prominent feature of excellence in the liberal arts, institutions and administrators across the country are increasingly asking David DeVries' question, "Where are the humanities in all this wealth of undergraduate research?"[2] After all, as professors in the humanities, we certainly affirm the inherent value of research in the fields of religion, philosophy, English, foreign languages, history, and the arts. We recognize that our courses and our fields make essential contributions to our collective knowledge and understanding of what it means to be human and that scholars in our field both help shape the world in which we live as well as maintain the "cultural memory of the human race."[3] Consequently, the low level of participation by religious studies faculty in the national movement around Undergraduate Research is more appropriately understood as an opportunity for growth rather than disinterest on the part of scholars of religion to engage in this form of pedagogy. For most professors, perhaps the issue is one of trying to figure out how to conceive of research projects at the undergraduate level that meet the criteria that have been defined by the Council on Undergraduate Research about what constitutes "Undergraduate Research."

The Council on Undergraduate Research (CUR) is the most prominent national professional organization dedicated to supporting and promoting "high-quality undergraduate student-faculty collaborative research and scholarship."[4] CUR has been definitive in the development, support, and growth of Undergraduate Research on campuses across the country, but it was not until 2009 that their structure expanded to include a division dedicated to the humanities. Begun in 1978 by a group of chemists from private liberal arts colleges, CUR has focused primarily on a model of Undergraduate Research that reflects the natural and social sciences. This history and commitment is evident both in their definition of Undergraduate Research as "an inquiry or investigation conducted by an undergraduate student that makes an original intellectual or creative contribution to the discipline" and in the way in which CUR defines the benefits of Undergraduate Research:

1) Enhances student learning through mentoring relationships with faculty.
2) Increases retention in the science, technology, engineering, and mathematics (STEM) pipeline.
3) Increases enrollment in graduate education, and provides effective career preparation.

4) Develops critical thinking, creativity, problem solving, and intellectual independence.

5) Develops an understanding of research methodology.

6) Promotes an innovation-oriented culture.[5]

While the first, third, fourth, and fifth benefits made perfect sense as we thought about our own pedagogical goals as professors of religious studies, the second and sixth were clearly linked to the history of the natural science traditions that began the movement toward Undergraduate Research. As scholars in the humanities and, even more specifically, as religious studies scholars begin to engage in the process of mentoring Undergraduate Research, one of the obstacles that we face is finding our way inside a culture and a mind-set about "what Undergraduate Research is" that has been almost exclusively defined by scientists rather than by humanities scholars. In some ways, we are entering a discourse that is alien to our own epistemological orientation. Given that the nature of research in the humanities involves individual scholars developing and pursuing research questions, the model of scholarly collaboration has not been the norm.

Humanities disciplines share an epistemological orientation that recognizes knowledge as socially constructed and shaped by culture, history, environment, class, race, gender, and other aspects of our social location. It is precisely because we recognize these issues and factors as essential to understanding our human condition that we engage in our respective disciplines. Our point is not that natural or social scientists disagree with these epistemological considerations (though some certainly would); rather, it is to say these considerations are not necessarily forefront as they conceive of and design research projects and questions. Our orientation to the question of "what constitutes knowledge" or, more pointedly, "what constitutes 'new' knowledge" is fundamentally different.

And this brings us back to CUR's definition of "what is Undergraduate Research?" When our Working Group first began to discuss the CUR definition, we were perplexed. What exactly did they mean by "original"? Had they forgotten to insert a comma between "original" and "intellectual" so that student work could either be an original OR an intellectual OR a creative contribution to the discipline? Or, were they expecting nineteen- and twenty-year-old college students to really make "original intellectual" contributions to our disciplines? As we pondered what Undergraduate Research would look like in our field, some of us commented that if we were not even sure we had yet made an "original intellectual" contribution to our disciplines, how could we possibly be expected to mentor an undergraduate to do this?

Over the course of our three years together as a Working Group, this question was one that we returned to time and time again. Since the question of what it means to make an original contribution to our field is something that many scholars confront in the context of their own research and writing, trying to conceive of how an undergraduate student might do this is certainly a valid question. After all, undergraduates lack the requisite years of training and experience that we have under our belts; they cannot possibly be expected to have read as widely or deeply as we have in our areas of expertise, much less understand how subfields and specialized topics relate to the field at large; and the capacity of most undergraduates to read primary texts in the original language is limited to nonexistent, as is their ability to read secondary material that is not available in English. Certainly, each of us could identify scores of other ways in which undergraduate students are limited in their capacity to engage in research projects that have the possibility of contributing anything "original" to our disciplines or to the larger field of religious studies.

In our early conversations we struggled with whether or not a definition that originated in the natural sciences was relevant or, even more important, useful in the humanities, and even more specifically for the field of religious studies. After all, was it necessary to simply "inherit" their definition and cede to the natural and social scientists the prerogative of defining this for us? On the one hand some of us thought that we should develop our own definition of Undergraduate Research, a definition that would be more appropriate to our field, to our epistemological orientations, to our own methodological approaches to research. On the other hand, our discussions about whether or not undergraduates were capable of original research prompted us to think more deeply and more critically about what we meant by Undergraduate Research in our field. Additionally, the recognition that our colleagues in the natural sciences were not claiming that undergraduates were making contributions to their disciplines that were equivalent to Ph.D. scientists prompted us to think more creatively about how CUR's definition not only might be relevant to our work in religious studies, but also might push us toward new ways of thinking about how undergraduate students in our field might engage in research at a level that is appropriate developmentally and that also moves beyond what Paulo Freire referred to as the banking model of educational theory.

What we found in our conversations was that there are a wide variety of ways that we, as mentors, engage undergraduate students in pursuing Undergraduate Research. As we discussed our different pedagogical approaches to mentoring Undergraduate Research, our recognition of the multiplicity of ways that it is possible to conduct Undergraduate Research in religious studies began to grow and expand. While we did not always agree about whether or not a particular research project fit our working definition of what qualifies as Undergraduate Research in religious studies, we grew to recognize the importance of flexibility and creativity on the part of mentors as well as under-graduates. Given our own recognition of the importance of a variety of interpre-tations of what constitutes "an original intellectual or creative contribution to the discipline," this chapter offers the insights and perspectives of several members of the Working Group in order to highlight some of the ongoing per-spectives and questions about what Undergraduate Research looks like in the field of religious studies.

A Fieldwork Approach

Rebecca Todd Peters, Elon University

Like many of my colleagues who mentor undergraduate students in Undergraduate Research in religious studies, I stumbled into it after being asked by students in my department to mentor their research projects during my second year as a full-time faculty member. My first group of students, in 2002, was part of an Arts and Humanities Fellows program, and the research project was the capstone requirement for their program. As I began to look into what sort of guidelines or standards were normative for Undergraduate Research in religious studies, I kept running into dead ends. After examining the resources available through the Council on Undergraduate Research (CUR) and spending some time searching for journal articles or other resources on the topic, it became clear to me that I was going to have to figure this out on my own. I set about trying to discern reasonable expectations for undergraduates with respect to research in religious studies. I knew that they were not capable of engaging in the kind of intellectual work that I do as a social ethicist, yet, it also seemed apparent that their work needed to move beyond my standard expectations for a research paper in a semester-long course. As I reflected on the CUR definition of Undergraduate Research as making an "original intellec-tual or creative contribution" to the discipline, I struggled with what kind of research project I could point my students toward that would fulfill this expectation.

As I thought about what my learning goals were for working with these students, I recognized that my primary objective was for the students to be engaged in an intellectual research project that allowed them to develop the following primary research skills: 1) working with primary documents, 2) anal-ysis and interpretation, and 3) drawing conclusions and developing concrete social policy or social ethical recommendations.[6] The question then became, how could I work with students to design a research project that facilitated the development of these research skills?

Ultimately, I settled on requiring the students to develop research projects that involved fieldwork or interviewing subjects (see chapter 7 for more detailed discussion of student projects that involve fieldwork). This methodological approach allowed students to develop their own primary documents (interviews or field notes) from which they were able to engage in their own original analysis and interpretation.

One of the first students that I worked with began her initial research process as a sophomore in a Research Methods course. Her initial interest was in examining how women respond and react to patriarchal biblical and liturgical language; like many of my students, her initial research questions arose out of her own experience. In her case, feelings of being excluded from the biblical narrative as a woman had a significant impact on her spirituality, and she wanted to explore this in an academic context. As a nineteen-year-old sophomore, she was not yet familiar with the body of literature in feminist theology that addresses many aspects of her initial question. Clearly, this topic did not have a hint of originality in it, but her work in that class introduced her to some of the basic literature on this issue and taught her how to develop a research agenda and how to construct an argument in a religious studies course. When she approached me the next year with the desire to continue researching the topic as part of a formal Undergraduate Research project, we talked about what she had learned in the initial semester of research and what additional reading she needed to do in order to develop an original research question. She did more extensive research on feminist theologies during her junior year; and by the end of the year, we had designed a much more substantial, interesting, and original research project. Her project involved interviewing twelve feminist pastors in North Carolina to examine how the feminist theology that they learned in seminary had shaped their approach to ministry and how they translated feminist theology into their churches. In reflecting on her experience, this student wrote:

> By interviewing feminist-identified women my objective has been to see how feminist theology has shaped their approach to ministry. My analysis seeks to offer an accurate portrayal of how feminist theology is being translated into a select group of Presbyterian churches in North Carolina, as well as to provide insight into how feminist theology continues to call for a transformation of ministry and the church. The findings of this research have drawn distinct parallels between women in ministry and women in academia. Further exploration into existing research on women in academia coupled with the results from my interviews shows that women in

professional fields are facing similar hierarchical issues as women in the church. I have found that feminist theology is calling for a restructuring of the typical patriarchal models of ministry that have forced women to exist in careers where the top positions were created for men.[7]

As with any sound research methodology, students do not always find the results that they anticipate. Another student I worked with had designed a research project that involved interviewing a group of mothers of young children to examine the ethical and social value of mothering and to analyze the ways in which the task of mothering contributes to the larger social good of a society. While the student and I were focused on examining how the women's actions of mothering contributed to a stronger and healthier society, we had not anticipated one of her most interesting findings: that the experience of becoming a mother also had a positive transformational impact on the self-identity of the women interviewed. Often, it is this recognition of a new insight or unexpected finding that helps students experience the real novelty and excitement of engaging in research.

By steering students toward projects that involve interviewing and fieldwork, I have been able to work with a number of students over the past nine years to develop significant Undergraduate Research projects that have allowed these students to make original and intellectual contributions to our field.

Defining Undergraduate Research in Religious Studies as a Separate Field

Robin Rinehart, Lafayette College

I know from my own experience as a mentor that Undergraduate Research in religious studies can be incredibly valuable and rewarding for both the student and the mentor. However, after many discussions with our Working Group, and my own reflections, I still have reservations about the criterion that Undergraduate Research in religious studies makes "an original intellectual or creative contribution to the field" unless we make certain qualifications in understanding that statement.

When our Working Group first met, I argued that it is perhaps best to apply the "original intellectual or creative contribution" criterion to the field only if we define that field as the body of research produced by undergraduates in religious studies. In other words, we encourage our students to produce the best possible work in comparison to their peers; except in unusual cases, it is not realistic to expect that their research will result in an article, for example, for a peer-reviewed journal. Students working with faculty mentors in the natural sciences may well contribute to research that results in coauthored journal articles; I think this is less likely for students doing research in humanities fields. If we conceptualize undergraduate work within religious studies as constituting its own field of study, then it is certainly the case that student work can be original or creative. I acknowledge and respect the skills our students bring to their research projects, and I learn from their work. Still, I have several reasons for my reluctance to embrace wholeheartedly the notion that undergraduates will produce original research that contributes to disciplinary knowledge.

First, it is hard not to be somewhat cynical about the way colleges and universities market themselves and the experiences they provide for students. Like the children of Lake Wobegon, every student is above average; every campus is a bastion of smiling diversity, with excellence and innovation in abundance at every turn. This idealized picture is of course the reality of a competitive higher-education environment in which many schools must promote themselves to attract a strong student body. Somehow, though, the idea of touting Undergraduate Research in religious studies as always resulting in an "original intellectual or creative contribution" to the field strikes me as altogether too much like the hyperbole of higher-education marketing.

Second, this criterion is potentially limiting. Some student projects are going to be better than others. One project may well exhibit originality and another may not. Sometimes the best students, for any number of reasons, may not produce the best work. And sometimes an average student can be inspired by a topic and write a paper or give a presentation that far surpasses our expectations. Yet in each case, whether the result is "an original intellectual or creative contribution" or not, the student's experience in completing the project can be profound.

Third, we need only look at the nature of research and publication in our field as scholars with Ph.D.s to see some of the potential pitfalls of asserting that all Undergraduate Research in religious studies will meet this criterion. There is plenty of work out there in our field that is important, significant, and useful but perhaps does not meet the CUR definition. But we depend on having that kind of work. And within our own careers, many of us can surely point to an article we published that was truly original and creative, but perhaps also another that may have built on other scholars' work or in some small way made an important addition to the body of work available, even if it wasn't groundbreaking. And most of us have likely had the experience of pursuing a research project that didn't work out or didn't lead to the results we expected. We learn from that experience nonetheless, and so can our students.

Finally, if we designate everything as "an original intellectual or creative contribution" to the field, then doesn't that statement lose some of its meaning? How can we acknowledge and celebrate our students' work when it truly is exceptional? Either we accept that some work will be more original or creative than other work, or we restrict the opportunity to pursue Undergraduate Research in religious studies to a tiny fraction of our students. I'd like to keep the opportunity available for as many students as possible and recognize the learning that results from the process of undertaking Undergraduate Research in religious studies.

Collaborative Research

Bernadette McNary-Zak, Rhodes College

When a faculty-driven research agenda incorporates students in constructive, meaningful ways, collaborative research can be a model wherein students participate in the processes and products of defining an original contribution to the discipline. Although there are barriers to collaborative work in the humanities, by adopting a form of the apprenticeship model of faculty-student collaboration common in the natural sciences, collaboration can occur. A form of the apprenticeship model provides faculty with an opportunity to undertake their research, and it provides students with an understanding of how faculty research makes a contribution to the discipline.

Several years ago, my department approved and offered a new upper-level seminar course, "Research in Religious Studies". The course contributes to departmental and college-wide efforts to institutionalize Undergraduate Research on our campus. It is intended to foster faculty collaboration and student engagement in research in our discipline. The first time the course was offered, four departmental faculty members paired with four students to research the public debate over the vetting of an ancient object as a religious relic. The research was designed to maximize opportunities for teaching and learning. Seminar sessions addressed issues pertaining to the area of inquiry. Student-faculty pairs took turns leading discussion on issues related directly to their specific research questions as each person's individual research and work progressed.

Faculty may be able to conduct research with each other, and with their students, by defining a research project around a single focus, topic, or theme that can be studied from a variety of methodological approaches. In order for

Undergraduate Research to be possible, participating faculty must be able to find a research project that students can be involved in, and they must be able to actively engage them in the research process.

Mentoring Departmental Honors Projects

Nadia M. Lahutsky, Texas Christian University

Most of my experience with mentoring Undergraduate Research projects has come in the form of working with students who are pursuing departmental honors, which has required of them a thesis. Typically students develop an idea for an area to pursue when they are juniors, and then the work of the project is largely done over the course of their senior year. They have sufficient time for ample reading and reflecting on the topic and for revising their initial research hunch, but they are definitely still going to be seriously deficient in the areas of original source languages, critical theory, and mastery of modern research languages. This lack is an obvious hindrance to working in these fields, and I do not recall in twenty years any honors thesis being done in biblical studies (although I recognize that there may be a variety of other reasons for this).

Religious studies faculty may be hesitant to encourage our undergraduate students to embark on research projects, but the campus enthusiasm for such activity has only grown over the last decade. Honors students at Texas Christian University have always been invited to present their research in April during Honors Week. Those presentations, early in the week, were first supplemented by an entire Friday of research presentations from students in the natural sciences and engineering. Only since 2005 has my college, AddRan College of Liberal Arts, done a similar day. I have come to believe that my college made a substantial contribution to the issue when a name was chosen for the event. It is called the AddRan Festival of Scholarship and Creativity.[8] Using the word *scholarship* accurately communicates that the students are presenting serious academic efforts, oftentimes investigating original sources and using appropriate interpretive theories, perhaps even looking at a topic in a way that had not occurred to anyone else previously. However, the choice not to label the work as *research* avoids the issue of original contribution to the larger body of scholarship, the full nature of which any particular undergraduate may not be completely aware.

The most recent honors thesis I mentored did manage to make an original contribution to the field. This student wanted to work on a project that would help him better understand his church, as he simultaneously sought to determine if he had a call to ministry. I am a historian; thus, it was natural for our initial conversations to focus on historical topics. He decided to look at a significant and relatively recent event, in fact, the event in which a movement finally acknowledged that it was an institution. In 1968, Disciples of Christ reached the culmination of about a decade of planning and officially became the Christian Church (Disciples of Christ). Yes, the irony of a group formalizing its structures in that year has been frequently noted! My student wasn't interested in irony, however; rather, he sought to analyze the *rhetoric* of the architects of Restructure, as the process has come to be known. In so doing, he was self-consciously pulling together elements from both of his majors.

Restructure has been heavily studied and written about, the object of several doctoral dissertations and a number of monographs and countless articles. These previous studies had been theological, ecclesiological, or even sociological. No one else had thought to put to those documents a lens consisting of styles of rhetoric and their effectiveness. He read those dissertations and monographs that had appeared prior to his research. He requested that the library staff retrieve for him from off-campus storage the relevant periodicals from 1960 through 1970; and he pored over them, looking for useful examples. We met on a biweekly basis to discuss the work he had been doing and to try to cut through knots as he encountered them. I could tell that he was developing a mastery of the personalities and the issues of the process, and I was especially delighted one day to hear him articulate a nuanced view of an event. I knew at that point he was going to do a fine job!

He did, in fact, produce a good thesis that made an original contribution. The "religion/history" half of his thesis was stronger than the "English/ rhetoric" portion. Nonetheless, he took various examples of rhetorical style and demonstrated their appearance in the theological/ecclesiological appeals made in the run-up to 1968. Additionally, he speculated about the extent to which the rhetoric employed may have been responsible for the extent of resistance to Restructure, contributing his own analysis to the already-myriad explanations for the number of congregations that refused to join this newly created institution.

My pride in his success was tempered just a bit as we reached the deadline for the final paper to be submitted to the appropriate offices. It turned out that he had—along the way—been in closer contact with me than with his rhetoric professor, creating some hard feelings. The deadline virtually overlapped with the last week before graduation, and too many other deadlines hit at the same time. The final paper was in better shape than he was by the end. I'll admit now, two years later, to a bit of disappointment (which I hope I effectively suppressed at the time) as he shared with me that the experience had convinced him to pursue the professional degree and ministry rather than the Ph.D. and teaching.

His seminary experience has confirmed for him the validity of his decision. I can see now that the kind of pastor he is becoming will be significantly informed by his experience of Undergraduate Research in religious studies. He probably won't need to be reminded by me to watch his rhetorical style.

Problem Based Learning as Avenue for Originality

Paul O. Myhre, Wabash Center for Teaching and Learning in Theology and Religion

Undergraduate Research projects designed largely around an inductive method using Problem Based Learning (PBL) can serve as a means toward collaborative research that allows students to develop original intellectual and creative contributions to the discourse of religious studies (see chapter 5 for an extended discussion of Problem Based Learning approaches to Undergraduate Research). Problem Based Learning focuses on identifying a primary question for investigation, discovering original documents that may be relevant, figuring out what additional research methods and skills are required to address the question, and thinking through what additional materials may be needed. Each of these tasks is well suited to the task of Undergraduate Research as mentors are able to incorporate students in each of these steps and help tailor specific research tasks that draw on a particular student's interests and strengths. With each successive investigation of primary and secondary archival documents, students are thrust into a world of questions that merit further consideration.

Archival research as a type of PBL invites students and teachers to collaborate in their exploration of research questions along open-ended pathways. Unlike a typical PBL, however, the student is not the primary determiner of what knowledge is required in order to answer the research question. Religious studies faculty need to be heavily involved as teacher, facilitator, mentor, and coach to aid the student in the process of identification and acquisition of required skills for answering the research question. Given the genuinely collaborative nature of PBL, it might be the case that any original research generated would not be the sole possession of an undergraduate student, but rather would be regarded as a cogenerated and co-owned original contribution by the professor and student.

The degree to which the Undergraduate Research project might contribute to original research and outcomes depends in part on the capacity of the student to stay with the project long enough to gain enough proficiency with the required materials and methods so as to be able to produce an original contribution. Undergraduate Research projects that seek an original contribution to the field of religious studies require a heavy investment of time in facilitating and mentoring. Students left to their own resources might hit on an original idea but would probably lack the requisite background knowledge, depth of research in religious studies, and experience with research and writing to bring it to fruition. Hence, faculty ought to regard themselves in partnership with the student on the research project—both in the research and writing of any report or essay on the findings.

The "Original Intellectual or Creative Contribution"

As faculty members in religious studies continue their involvement in and commitment to Undergraduate Research, they will need to consider seriously the goal set by CUR of making an "original intellectual or creative contribution" to the discipline. As the perspectives presented here demonstrate, this goal raises important questions about learning outcomes and student abilities. It draws our attention to structural considerations, the research process, and time limits. It reminds us of the significance of the mentoring role and institutional support. While these perspectives illumine some of the parameters of the conversation about this goal, they also emphasize a lack of consensus that may be associated with the nature of our discipline.

The task of Undergraduate Research in religious studies is to teach, mentor, and apprentice students into the habits of intellectual inquiry that will allow them to learn how to ask questions, to know how to discern which questions are worth pursuing, and to know how their questions fit into a larger theoretical landscape in religious studies and the humanities. Furthermore, solid mentoring will teach students how to design a research process or methodology that allows them to answer their question. If Undergraduate Research serves to introduce students to research in religious studies, then the goal of making "an original intellectual or creative contribution" is bound to those ways of knowing, to those ways we construct knowledge, in our discipline.[9] So, for example, in some cases, like those described by Peters and McNary-Zak, Undergraduate Research may be involved in the gathering of primary source material as the data from which to work; in other cases, like those described by Lahutsky and Myhre, Undergraduate Research may be involved in applying new approaches to existing sources.

In all cases, Undergraduate Research in religious studies employs rational and critical processes of inquiry. In these terms, the study of religion through Undergraduate Research employs methodological approaches that conform to disciplinary standards. As Rinehart and Lahutsky remind us, there are intellectual consequences for the student who participates in the act of constructing knowledge in religious studies through Undergraduate Research. The significance of contextual influences upon a student means that one's location within the broader world impacts the questions one raises, the approaches one uses, what one sees as a meaningful research agenda, and the goals and means through which one conducts and evaluates research. Questions and commitments concerning the origins, formation, and validation of knowledge necessarily shape one's interpretation of an "original intellectual or creative contribution" in religious studies.

Despite the lack of consensus regarding what constitutes an "original intellectual or creative contribution" in the perspectives presented above, it is the case that when faculty and students participate in Undergraduate Research in religious studies, they help define those modes of inquiry valued by religious studies and other humanities disciplines. In the process, they further clarify the distinctiveness of Undergraduate Research in the humanities and articulate goals and strategies for preparing students to make a contribution to the construction of knowledge in the discipline.

Student Reflection on Making an Original Contribution

Shelton Oakley

The Undergraduate Research process—from beginning to end—demanded a degree of attention and ownership that stretched me as a student. With an academic comfort zone defined by essays, course-required books and a generous list of questions provided by the professor, the process of personalized research expanded my ability to think critically. Creating an original idea to research proved to be the most difficult, yet most important step. After taking numerous religious studies courses and absorbing brilliant ideas from different scholars, I was challenged by the initial task of choosing an undiscovered topic—one on which to provide new insights. Moreover, exploring what already existed under the discipline of religious studies while searching for new ideas that would spark my interest called for thinking outside the box about what Undergraduate Research encompasses. In the end, the voice of everyday people through interviews became my most significant source. The challenge extends beyond finding an original idea, however, with every step in the research process interconnected and decisively thought through by the student. From honing a thesis and determining what research is applicable to finally laying out the format through which you hope to successfully convey your argument and sources, beginning to end, the research and final outcome belong solely to the student.

NOTES

1. Walter H. Capps, *Religious Studies: The Making of a Discipline* (Minneapolis: Fortress Press, 1995), 331.

2. David N. DeVries, "Undergraduate Research in the Humanities: An Oxymoron?" *CUR Quarterly* 21, no. 4 (June 2001): 154.

3. Ibid.

4. See http://www.cur.org, "Council on Undergraduate Research Mission Statement."

5. See http://www.cur.org/factsheet.html, "CUR Fact Sheet."

6. Of course, I have a host of secondary research skills that I expect students to master, including developing a research question, creating a research agenda, critical reading skills, and sophisticated and nuanced writing. But it is my expectation that these types of skills are foundational to all methodological approaches to Undergraduate Research and would be shared by most of my colleagues regardless of how they answered the question, "What constitutes an original intellectual or creative contribution to the field of Religious Studies?"

7. Erin Keys, reflections on her research project titled, "Impact of Feminist Theology on the Life and Thought of the Christian Church," http://facstaff.elon.edu/rpeters/Mentoring/AHScholars.html#EK (accessed June 17, 2009).

8. Unfortunately, at the 2009 opening of the festival, the Dean welcomed everyone to the AddRan Festival of Research and Creativity. Maybe next year we'll need to provide him with his script.

9. In Undergraduate Research, our students may begin to learn these ways of knowing by designing and completing research that understands the term *religion*, in the words of Sam Gill, "as designating an academically constructed rubric that identifies the arena for common discourse inclusive of all religions as historically and culturally manifest". Sam Gill, "The Academic Study of Religion," *Journal of the American Academy of Religion* 62, no. 4 (Winter 1994): 965.

3

Mentoring Undergraduate Research

Lynn R. Huber and John R. Lanci

> Tell me, I forget
> Show me, I remember
> Involve me, I understand.
> —Ancient Chinese Proverb

At its essence, good teaching is about relationships. Even more than the successful transfer of information, effective education involves the forging of relationships between students and their faculty. Research has consistently demonstrated a positive correlation between strong faculty-student interaction and educational success, from grades to graduation with honors and admission to graduate school.[1] And if effective teaching is about fostering relationships, good mentoring has been shown to be among the most highly effective of instructional relationships.[2] Some of the benefits of mentoring (academic and nonacademic) include "honed thinking skills, enhanced creativity, increased self-esteem, improved skills."[3] The number one recommendation made by the Boyer Commission in its list "Ten Ways to Change Undergraduate Education" was to assert, "learning is based on discovery guided by mentoring rather than on the transmission of information."[4] A recent study suggests that the mentoring relationship experienced in the context of Undergraduate Research led a higher number of students to pursue graduate education than students who had not participated in Undergraduate Research.[5]

There are as many ways to mentor students as there are faculty inter-ested in doing it; no one style or theory of mentoring has gained anything close to universal acceptance, despite the publication of a great deal of research. Nonetheless, there is little disagreement that it is the process of student engagement in formulating research questions and answers in close relationship with a faculty mentor that draws many students to Undergraduate Research. In what follows, we will touch briefly on a number of questions associated with the dynamics of collaboration between undergraduate stu-dents and faculty. To begin, how should we understand what it means to mentor? While the mentoring experience varies depending on particular cir-cumstances, the relationships that are created evolve and change over time; what are some of the stages or shifts we can expect within the mentoring relationship? How might faculty prepare for the mentoring experience? What are some of the issues that arise when we seek to work closely with undergraduates, often outside the usual structures of the classroom? And are there any insights that we in theology and the study of religion might bring to wider institutional discussions about the nature of mentoring and collaboration?

We come to this conversation from distinct stages in our careers: John is a tenured professor at a small Catholic liberal arts college late in his career, and Lynn recently received tenure at a midsized university that focuses upon the liberal arts and engaged learning. Thus, while John has mentored a variety of students in a number of different teaching contexts, Lynn is beginning the process of mentoring students and has done so within the confines of the Undergraduate Research program at her institu-tion. Specifically, John has mentored a number of students through his uni-versity's summer research program, experiences that have even yielded joint publications. Lynn's mentoring experiences have been through pro-grams in which she has worked with students on projects that extended over multiple semesters with final products ranging from presentations, to Undergraduate Research journal articles, and honors theses. Additionally, we come to the conversation about mentoring with different experiences and expectations based upon our genders, ages, and regional backgrounds, just to name a few factors shaping our teaching identities. In spite of these differences, we share a commitment to thinking about how mentoring can be transformative practice for mentee and mentor alike. In particular, we are drawn to mentoring on account of its potential for collaboration and transformation—the transformation of students into scholars and teachers into collaborators.[6]

Mentoring Is Intentional, Risky, and Reciprocal (John)

However one defines academic mentoring—as a faculty member who provides emotional and psychological support, who assists the student with professional or intellectual development, or who functions as a role model—we suggest that three interrelated characteristics separate it out from the other roles faculty fill:

1. Effective mentoring is *intentional*.[7] Good mentors spend time and effort discovering how to mentor; they understand mentoring to be difficult, but rewarding, and they remain self-aware concerning the process, the "journey," that is mentoring.[8]

2. Mentoring *involves risks* unlike those faculty face in other aspects of their jobs.[9] Mentoring raises issues of boundary formation; the mentor spends a great deal of time with the mentee, and the relationship between the two can, and often does, legitimately extend into realms more personal than we may have expected. Mentoring challenges our self-understanding as dispensers of received wisdom and information; it invites us to be a guide to students, but, particularly in Undergraduate Research projects, we may find ourselves functioning as partners or colleagues with our students. Mentoring demands that we allow the students room to grow and develop their own ideas and their own self-understanding as scholars, and this means that sometimes—particularly in the later stages of the mentoring journey— even at the undergraduate level, faculty may begin to find the mentee guiding *us*.[10]

3. This mutuality is what sets mentoring apart from the other roles we take on as faculty: mentoring is *reciprocal*. As we will see in the next section, the mentor-mentee relationship is "a complex interactive process" in which both parties pass through a series of stages.[11] The complexity of this process is due in great part to the reciprocity that is at its heart. Reciprocity is widely considered to be "a fundamental component of mentoring relationships, part of the very definition of what it means to mentor and be mentored."[12] There is no one "correct" way to mentor Undergraduate Research students, as numerous factors influence the character of this teaching relationship. We suggest, though, that at its essence mentoring that is intentional and involves some level of risk and an expectation of reciprocity will provide a highly effective learning opportunity for students.

Two Steps Forward, One Step Back: Stages and Experiences
in the Mentoring Relationship (Lynn)

Scholars typically describe the mentoring relationship as unfolding in a linear fashion and as progressing through a set of stages, such as "initiation," "cultivation," "transformation," and "separation."[13] The notion that the mentoring relationship unfolds in stages, even if we qualify this with the caveat that the stages overlap, belies the fact that each mentoring relationship has unique contours, some relationships unfold in a linear fashion, while others circle around a research question in a way that resembles more of a spiral.

While the notion that there are particular stages may be misleading, mentoring relationships often involve a period of initiation or stages of beginnings. The formal start of the mentoring relationship, when both parties come together to set mutual goals and expectations, is one sort of beginning stage.[14] In my experience, the beginnings of mentoring relationships are not always well defined: sometimes student and mentor will begin a line of inquiry together in a classroom setting.[15] For example, one of the honors students I mentored began thinking about a topic for her thesis in the context of a course she took with me on art and the Bible and only approached me about serving as her official thesis mentor about a year and a half after the course. My mentoring of this student began before I even recognized it as a definable relationship. In contrast, some mentoring experiences begin more clearly, when a student comes to your door at the beginning of a research project, asking you to help define a question and a project.

Whether the mentoring relationship emerges unexpectedly or in a more clear fashion, being intentional as a mentor suggests the importance of articulating expectations early on, at the beginning of the relationship. This ideally involves a certain amount of self-reflection by both participants, in which they individually and jointly articulate what they want out of the experience in terms of process and outcome. Although we do not want to stifle a student's academic enthusiasm, it is the responsibility of the mentor to set realistic expectations and to encourage the student to adopt a similar posture. One of the questions to consider in this stage is, how much time can both parties realistically devote to this project and this working relationship? Be honest with your students about the time and effort you expect to be put forth. This honesty at the beginning of the process not only helps prepare your students for what they are signing up for and gives them the chance to succeed in meeting your expectations, but also establishes a precedent of honesty that can be a valuable thing if and when the Undergraduate Research process encounters difficulties.

Additionally, at the beginning of mentoring relationships mentees may be quite vulnerable or unsure of their skills.[16] At this point, there may be a special need for understanding and patience; however, as students become more confident in their abilities and more trusting of the mentor, the relationship between the two matures and the mentor can challenge the student more effectively.

Ideally, this period of setting expectations is when student and professor work to articulate the primary research question and begin the process of getting to know each other's work styles and preferences. It is important to underscore the value of mutuality in this experience. In Undergraduate Research, the idea behind the project and the process itself ideally belongs to both mentor and mentee. This is one of the things that makes Undergraduate Research different from other forms of undergraduate learning experiences: when the student is an integral part of articulating the question and research plan, it engenders a sense of true ownership of the project.

As the relationship and the project progress there are subsequent initiations or "beginnings" that occur. At different transitions within the research itself and even at transitional periods due to the academic calendar, mentor and mentee may find themselves resetting expectations and learning new aspects of each other's work styles. For example, when the project moves from an investigatory stage, when the student and faculty mentor work to get a sense of the field, into a stage which is more writing focused, a new set of questions and complications can surface as the mentor and mentee learn each other's writing preferences, styles, and processes. New expectations have to be articulated, just as the mentor and mentee set expectations as they began the relationship and the project. Attending to these subsequent beginnings is part of "cultivating" the mentoring relationship over a period of time.[17] Especially in long-term projects, such as those that take a year or more, as a mentor and mentee move through the Undergraduate Research project, they may return over and over again to certain stages and processes.

Many use the agricultural metaphor of cultivation to describe the mentoring relationship.[18] In so doing, the mentee is depicted as one who is being cultivated by the mentor. The mentor "prepares" the mentee, like one would prepare soil, and "feeds" the student by giving the information needed to "grow" intellectually. Eventually, the student yields the "fruit," or the research project, but it is primarily a result of the mentor's cultivation or work. We propose a second use of the metaphor of mentoring as cultivation: imagine the mentoring relationship itself as something that is cultivated, through a common research project. The mentor and mentee work together to nurture the relationship as they nurture the project. Both participants cultivate the field or do the work of the research, even though the mentor may often take on the role of sharing techniques or approaches to the mentee. However, the mentee may bring a perspective to the project that the mentor had not anticipated, if we imagine the mentor relationship in this way. Envisioning the mentoring relationship in this way means that the fruit of the project is the result of the work of both parties. This latter way of envisioning cultivation imagines the collaborative aspect of the mentoring relationship, one of our shared motivations for engaging in Undergraduate Research. In practice, most mentoring relationships involve imagining cultivation in both ways, as mentor cultivating the student and the pair cultivating their relationship and project. Moreover, often the point at which an Undergraduate Research relationship shifts from a relationship in which the mentor leads to a situation in which participants work together in a mutual way is recognized only in retrospect.

Learning to take risks is part of the Undergraduate Research mentoring experience. This is true not only for the student but also for the faculty member who chooses to work with a student on an original project. This unpredictability is something our students have to learn, and our role as mentors is to help them learn how to move through the unexpected results of research and even to see the unexpected results as an opportunity. For some of us, part of the enjoyment that comes with mentoring in Undergraduate Research is that each experience requires its own plan of action, a research agenda tailored to the topic, the participants, and the parameters of the project. This means that one cannot "stage-manage" the unfolding of the mentoring relationship, as new issues and questions arise throughout the project.

In spite of the unpredictable nature of mentoring relationships, they do typically come to some sort of end or transition at which the experience is no longer defined as a mentor-mentee relationship. Some Undergraduate Research projects end with the completion of a paper or a presentation of research. Some end as students graduate or move on to another stage in their college career. However the relationship ends, these endings can be as full of emotion as other types of closures or endings.[19] Students and faculty alike may be excited about the product but experience loss and even frustration as the working relationship comes to a close.[20] This can be especially true for the student, if the Undergraduate Research experience has been a transformative educational experience. As in other types of endings, acknowledging the complexity of emotion can be one way of dealing with the ending of the mentoring experience. Additionally, the mentor might consider a final meeting with the student that anticipates the contours of the new relationship, such as a simple conversation over coffee about the new directions the mentee is taking independently or under the guidance of another.

As one might expect in teaching and learning situations that are built around the distinctive relationships between a unique faculty person and a similarly unique student, the mentoring relationship is understood, characterized and embodied in a variety of ways. It is the total experience of moving through the research process, including the stops, starts, and seeming reversals that occur in every relationship and that occur within every research project, that comprises the Undergraduate Research mentoring relationship.[21]

Why Mentor? (John)

Strong student-faculty interaction "has significant positive correlations with every academic attainment outcome," from grades to postgraduate enrollment, as well as all areas of intellectual and personal growth.[22] Richard Light's study of hundreds of Harvard undergraduates confirms the importance given by the Boyer Commission to faculty-student interaction, noting that "students who get the most out of college ... organize their time to include interpersonal activities with faculty members, or with fellow students, built around substantive, academic work."[23] But as Laurent A. Daloz has said, "We teach for ourselves as well," and faculty benefit in many ways from the experience of mentoring.[24]

Mentoring Is Personally Satisfying

Studies have shown that the close cooperation of mentor and mentee is highly satisfying to both.[25] Working closely with one or two students offers us the opportunity to see close-up the effect we have on student learning, and this sense of accomplishment can renew our enthusiasm for our work.[26] W. Brad Johnson identifies what he calls the "creative synergy" that can develop between mentor and mentee and "trigger a creative renaissance in the lives of faculty members."[27]

Mentoring Can Benefit our Research Agendas

Mentees approach our work with different perspectives and insights, and these can stimulate our own thinking in new and productive ways. We might become aware of gaps in our knowledge or connections we did not see before; we are forced to develop new ways to explain our project to the neophyte now working with us, and in the process we can clarify and sharpen our ability to promulgate our work to a wider audience (for more discussion of how undergraduate projects can align with faculty research agendas, see chapter 5). And even when a student does not control the languages or other technical matters involved, extra eyes, ears, and hands may assist one in the gathering and analysis of primary material. Working with students in areas that complement our research can even help us imagine new directions for our research. Lynn, for example, found that reading she did with a student doing an honors thesis on art and religion has provided important material for her own current research project, and John recently coauthored a successful grant proposal with a student who was his teaching assistant and suggested a new approach to material he had been developing.

Mentoring Enhances Teaching

Working as a mentor with students offers us a window into their perception of the world, and this can improve our ability to connect with the rest of our students in more conventional classroom settings. When a student and I are struggling over a research problem together—how best to prompt first-year students to articulate their experience of spirituality, for instance—we are forced to listen carefully to each other; this often leads to a deeper understanding on both sides, and this understanding is transferable to my mentee's peers.[28]

Mentoring Can Link Us to Our Professional Community

When we mentor Undergraduate Research, we introduce students to the issues and concerns of the community of scholars in religious studies and theology, and some of our mentees will go on to become members of that community in their own right. Those whom we introduced to the field then become part of our own network of relationships, yielding professional benefits for years to come.[29]

Mentoring Can Enhance Our Professional Stature

No matter how our institutions evaluate a commitment to mentoring with respect to tenure or promotion, a reputation as an effective mentor can enhance one's stature—and thus, effectiveness—at one's place of work and in the field as a whole. Good mentors attract good students, and, particularly at small liberal arts colleges, this is not lost on those who market higher education. Excellence in teaching is a powerful recruiting tool, and for many schools the opportunity for students to engage in Undergraduate Research and other engaged pedagogies that involve close contact between faculty and students cannot help but enhance the position of those who can mentor effectively.

Preparing to Mentor (John)

Who we are—our attitude, training, and personality—influences how we will mentor. As a result, mentoring looks very different "on the ground," depending on who it is that is doing it. Lynn has already alluded to some of the interpersonal skills necessary for effective mentoring: flexibility, intentionality, and patience. Other personal attributes and skills include honesty, humor, empathy, compassion, competency, and an assortment of human relational skills like good listening, assertiveness, and the ability to trust.[30] But there are a number of other factors that all mentors of Undergraduate Research should consider as they prepare for this work having to do with the institutional setting for mentoring: the kinds of students we mentor, the projects we mentor, and the theories of learning we espouse.

The Institutional Setting

An effective mentoring program is a proven way to make a college more marketable and to attract more gifted and motivated students.[31] Such programs can be magnets for donations from alumni/ae and other benefactors. However, it is important to ascertain the nature and actual depth of the institutional commitment and to align one's expectations with those of one's college or university. Beneficial as mentoring one's best students might be, if the college reward system (tenure and promotion, in particular) does not acknowledge this work as crucial to its mission, one may not be able to devote as much time to mentoring as one might like, since other activities will take priority. When considering mentorship as a significant part of one's work, it is important to discover if one's institution shares one's own conviction about the importance and potential with respect to mentoring.[32]

Whom Will You Mentor?

Studies have demonstrated that mentoring positively affects the learning of any kind of student. One must consider how one decides whom to mentor. Does the mission statement of the institution place priorities on minority students? Is there a need for mentoring in the gender studies program? Is the college moving into new areas, such as service learning, that could use some individual attention of faculty? Has the university made a commitment to retain first-generation college students? What are your own preferences: Would you prefer to work with a student you already know, or would you accept one on someone else's recommendation? Will you do your best mentoring with someone of the same gender, or is that not an important concern? Do you have gifts or interests best employed in service of students who need extra attention or educational accommodations? Or are you more attracted to working with the best and the brightest? Wherever you land with respect to these questions, it is better to do some thinking and perhaps some research into local institutional commitments as one considers the possibility of mentoring.

What Research Project to Mentor?

The type of research to be done must match the skill set of the student. As noted elsewhere in this volume, this is a particular problem for Undergraduate Research in religious studies, in which so much of our work depends on proficiency in languages and methodologies from a diverse array of academic fields. It is important to underscore the importance of thinking honestly and realistically about what sorts of skills and areas of inquiry you, the faculty person, can really help the student navigate in a thorough and critical fashion. While it may be tempting to do so, to take on a student whose research interests are tangential to your own can be difficult and can result in a questionable outcome.

Our Role in the Mentor/Mentee Relationship

No matter what the institutional situation, training, or personal preferences involved, one's style of mentoring will depend on how one understands student learning. Recent pedagogical research is clear that the best results are achieved when students play an active role in the process of their own learning. We suggest that despite the likelihood that most academics working today were spawned by a system that prized "stand and deliver" lecture classes, the most effective mentoring challenges one whenever possible to check one's need for control of the learning process at the proverbial door.

To actuate the learning-rich reciprocity of mentoring—and its potential for transforming both parties involved—one must be prepared to relinquish some (perhaps most) of our traditional faculty control. In this it is similar to the role the teacher plays in other forms of active learning: we encourage students to think for themselves, to outgrow the need for close supervision and guidance. But with this comes freedom for the student—and for the Undergraduate Research project—to miss expectations or perhaps even to fail.

While we may find ourselves stumbling into a situation that calls for mentoring, our response will effectively promote student learning only to the degree that we prepare ourselves for the experience. Given the expense of time and resources, and as we shall see in the next section, given the potential for difficulties that may arise as traditional boundaries and responsibilities shift, honest self-reflection as we consider our calling as mentors is critical.

Issues in Mentoring: Power and Boundaries (Lynn)

The opportunity for developing a close working relationship between mentor and mentee, a relationship that allows us a chance to glimpse the full potential of the teaching vocation, draws many of us to Undergraduate Research. Similarly, this is one of the factors that attracts students to such a labor-intensive endeavor and one of the things they find the most valuable in Undergraduate Research. Typically characterized by one-on-one guidance and growing mutuality, this relationship has the potential for positive transformation and intellectual empowerment.

As described above, mentoring relationships may result in the transformation of student into scholar and the mentoring relationship into a collaborative learning/research opportunity. In addition, mentoring in Undergraduate Research has the possibility of contributing to the positive transformation of many academic environments, especially predominantly white institutions, into places where diverse populations are accepted and can succeed. What research has been done on mentoring in relation to race and gender, suggests that students of color and women generally benefit from formal and informal mentoring.[33] For instance, mentoring relationships have the potential to validate the presence of minority students within an academic setting, as well as to introduce these students to the ins and outs of research. As Margaret Scisney-Matlock and John Matlock describe, students of color often point to the lack of relationships with faculty as a sign of their marginalization within an academic institution. Mentoring can increase the performance of traditionally underrepresented groups, regardless of the racial or ethnic background or gender of the mentor.[34] In this way, mentoring Undergraduate Research can be transformative in social terms, as well as in individual terms.

The mentoring relationship also involves a blurring of traditional student-teacher boundaries. The bulk of work done in a mentoring relationship is one-on-one and may involve meeting outside of traditional class times, such as during evenings or on weekends. This shifting of boundaries, ideally, happens in more intangible ways as the student is involved in shaping research questions and trajectories. Moreover, as the student progresses through the difficult task of undergraduate research there are bound to be emotional exchanges, whether out of frustration or intellectual excitement. I've had a student weep in my office because she "just doesn't get it," and I've had a student spontaneously embrace me as he heard good news in response to his Undergraduate Research work. While these things may happen in a more traditional student-teacher relationship, these events can be more emotionally charged than they would be in a traditional teaching scenario. Similarly, as a mentor, I became more emotionally connected to my students, cringing and even becoming defensive when I hear another faculty member criticize an aspect of my mentee's research and bursting with pride when a student's final paper is published in an Undergraduate Research journal.

More important, while the mentoring relationship has the potential to empower students, one must be especially conscious of the fact that the power imbalance inherent in faculty-student interactions endures, even as it changes, within the mentoring relationship. While we strive for mutuality in our working relationship with undergraduate researchers, we necessarily possess more power in the relationship than the mentee, by virtue of our experience, expertise, and faculty position. Far from disappearing, the power imbalance in the mentoring relationship can become even more complicated as the relationship develops. Undergraduate Research experiences demand that students take more risks than in a typical classroom setting, thereby possibly making students even more vulnerable to the power exercised by the mentor. Johnson notes that students may be particularly vulnerable in the beginning stages of the mentoring relationship when there is a tendency to idealize and even a desire to become enmeshed with the mentor.[35] Among other things, as the relationship grows between mentor and mentee, the mentee can become tempted to "perform" primarily for the sake of the mentor and not for the sake of the project or not out of a personal desire to learn. This can create a scenario that is potentially difficult and even exploitative for both mentor and mentee.

The potential for blurring of boundaries requires increased attention and awareness on the part of the mentor to the fact that while mentoring has a personal dimension, it is still unequivocally a professional relationship. The potential for abuse or exploitation includes, but is not limited to, sexual abuse or harassment. In a highly charged academic setting in which a student's work might be interpreted as indicative of the professor's academic work, there exists the possibility of emotional abuse and manipulation.[36] For instance it is possible for a mentor to unintentionally prompt a mentee to fight the mentor's own political or academic battles. Ideally, we should guard against making mentees into our mouthpieces or allowing them to become collateral damage in skirmishes with our colleagues.

The mentoring relationship can also be ethically compromised when it becomes a context for either the student or the faculty person to address personal or emotional issues. Clearly, mentoring is not a substitute for a counseling relationship; however, the shifting boundaries of the relationship and a mentor or mentee's good intentions make this an easy thing for some to forget. If the problems are those of the mentor, he or she has a responsibility to seek help and to be mindful of not bringing these into the mentoring relationship. Likewise, if the mentee brings emotional, relational, or family problems into the mentoring conversation, a mentor should be empathetic but guide the student to a qualified professional.

As mentors we are responsible for setting boundaries and controlling behaviors and attitudes that might cross the line into abuse. In *On Being a Mentor*, Johnson reminds us that mentors should attend to the ethical obligations of our profession as teachers, including obligations to do no harm to our students and to work toward their personal growth as individuals and scholars.[37] Being a mentor requires us to be cognizant of the balance between listening to our students' concerns, questions, and issues and knowing when to set limits. Suffice it to say, mentoring is not for the faculty person who wants to avoid difficult conversations or for the individual who likes working relationships to be simple and straightforward.

Mentoring Undergraduate Research in Religious Studies and Theology

More than most other fields of inquiry, the study of religion and theology impacts the personal experience of a significant number of our students in a direct fashion. For many of us, it is a rare Undergraduate Research project that does not include some desire on the part of students to reflect on wider questions of religious values and the history of religious practice, often motivated by their own personal experience. Many people in our fields were introduced to the academic study of religion while pursuing studies in pastoral care or ministry (both of us did). Negotiating the boundaries between the two professional fields—academic and pastoral—is complicated and can be a challenge particularly when presented with students who are asking questions better addressed by a pastor than a mentor. We suggest that the tension that can be generated in situations like this has taught most of us, even those with little interest or training in pastoral theology, to be acutely aware of our location and purpose as educators. Through this heightened sense of our purpose and awareness of the power dynamics of our interactions with students, we who study religion and theology are well placed to contribute to the wider conversation about mentoring in Undergraduate Research, particularly in the humanities.

One of the main things that the discipline of religious studies can contribute to conversations about mentoring in Undergraduate Research is the recognition that researchers (both faculty and students) are often stakeholders in the topics and questions they pursue. Feminist theologians and scholars of religion in particular (e.g., Elisabeth Schüssler Fiorenza) have underscored the fact that researchers are drawn to lines of inquiry because we have some sort of investment in that field of inquiry, whether we are conscious of it or not. Not only are the results of our research shaped by our ideological commitments and concerns, but also the very questions we ask are molded by these same interests. Work in our field demands that we teach our students to be self-critical, exploring how their interests and social locations shape their research questions and agendas.[38]

How we locate ourselves as mentors in relationship to students is another area of pedagogical interest to which the study of religion can make a substantial contribution. The pedagogical role of the scholar and academic mentor must shift from being the gatekeeper of knowledge, the purveyor of authoritative information to one who facilitates a community's conversation, exerting little control over the proceedings while helping the community place its insights within the wider tradition. In this schema, the expert becomes a companion on the journey, a resource to aid the community in the discernment it must do as it owns its situation in the world. The scholar proffers an invitation to members of the community to step into the center of the circle of discernment as a legitimate participant.[39]

All of this leads us to one last thought. In the field of religious studies, as in some other fields, we are continually reminded that research is not done in a vacuum. This is something that we can and should remind our mentees. Our research can have implications for and impacts upon the world outside of the academy. The historical roots of our field in theological training point to the fact that academic research is often done in service to a community or entity outside of the academy. While many of us find our academic homes less tied to formal religious bodies, many still understand their research as something that should be held accountable to given communities, whether those communities are constructed through religious identity or some other social identity, such as ethnic, cultural, gendered, or sexual identities. Even when we do not explicitly articulate our accountability to a particular community, our research necessarily takes a side in support of a particular ideology, as feminist and liberationist scholars remind us. Thus, we do our best work when we engage in at least some form of critical self-reflection upon how our identities and commitments shape our research and its political assumptions.[40] This is something that, as mentors, we can model for our students. Moreover, both we and our mentees can encourage research programs in general to think seriously about the importance of incorporating critical self-reflection into all types of undergraduate research.

Student Reflection on Mentoring

Erin Keys

Working with a mentor is an essential part of learning the art of an academic discipline. For one, you have someone who genuinely believes in your potential as a scholar. The support provided by an academic mentor enables the student to discover the potential within oneself. In my own experience I was not a student who ever saw myself as a "scholar." Only after my mentor took an interest in my class work, and we began to work together, did I become aware of the possibility I had within myself to engage in critical thought.

Within the scope of critical thought also came original thought. "What are you interested in?" my mentor asked me. In retrospect I don't think that question gets asked of undergraduates very often. Typically the scope of what you are interested in rarely extends beyond the broad category of your major and even then is focused on what job you will have after your degree is completed. To realize I could merge my interests into the larger academic discipline was truly eye opening. In my case this began by asking a question about the way Christian women relate to a male-centric scripture and evolved into a final project examining the ways feminist theology has impacted the lives of female PCUSA pastors.

NOTES

1. Alexander W. Astin, *What Matters in College?* (San Francisco: Jossey-Bass, 1993), 381; Laurent A. Daloz, *Mentor: Guiding the Journey of Adult Learners* (San Francisco: Jossey-Bass, 1999), 239.

2. Brad W. Johnson, *On Being a Mentor: A Guide for Higher Education Faculty.* (London: Routledge, 2007), 7; Elaine Seymour, et al., "Establishing the Benefits of Research Experiences for Undergraduates in the Sciences," *Science Education* 88, no. 4 (2004): 509; Lila Guterman, "What Good Is Undergraduate Research, Anyway?" *The Chronicle for Higher Education* 53, no. 50(August 17, 2007): 11.

3. Mitchell Malachowski. "The Mentoring Role in Undergraduate Research Projects." *CUR Quarterly* 12 (1996): 93.

4. Boyer Commission on Educating Undergraduates in the Research University, *Reinventing Undergraduate Education: A Blueprint for America's Research Universities* (Stony Brook, NY: State University of New York, 1998), 15. In response to legislators' and academic administrators' concerns in the 1980s, the Carnegie Foundation for the Advancement of Teaching funded a commission managed until his death by Ernest

Boyer, to report on the state of undergraduate education in the United States and to suggest recommendations for long-range improvements.

5. Russell S. Hathaway, Biren A. Nagda, and Sandra Gregerman, "The Relationship of Undergraduate Research Participation to Graduate and Professional Education Pursuit: An Empirical Study," *Journal of College Student Development* 43, no. 5 (2002): 614–31.

6. As this chapter is itself a collaboration, a word of explanation is necessary. In keeping with the style of the rest of this book, we include references to our own experience. To keep disruptive references to "Lynn" and "John" to a minimum, we have flagged which of us was lead author for each section. The reader can assume that any reference to personal pedagogical experience is that of the lead author, though all sections are the product of a thorough collaborative effort.

7. Johnson, *On Being a Mentor*, 3.

8. Daloz, *Mentor*, 18 and passim.

9. Robert Aubrey and Paul M. Cohen. *Working Wisdom* (San Francisco: Jossey-Bass, 1995), 49.

10. Mary L. Otto, "Mentoring: An Adult Developmental Perspective." *New Directions for Teaching and Learning* 57 (1994): 15–24; Angela Brew, "Teaching and Research: New Relationships and Their Implications for Inquiry Based Teaching and Learning in Higher Education," Higher 14–17; Daloz, *Mentor*, 244.

11. Cheryl N. Carmin, "Issues in Research on Mentoring: Definitional and Methodological," *International Journal of Mentoring* 2, no. 2 (1988): 10.

12. Wendelyn J. Shore, Toyokawa Teru and Dana D. Anderson, "Context-Specific Effects on Reciprocity in Mentoring Relationships: Ethical Implications," *Mentoring & Tutoring: Partnership in Learning* 16.1 (2008), 17; Brew, "Teaching and Research," 15; Johnson, *On Being a Mentor*, 12–13; Seymour et al., "Establishing the Benefits," 510.

13. Malachowski, "The Mentoring Role," 91–93. See also, Kathy E. Kram, "Phases of the Mentor Relationship," *Academy of Management Journal* 26, no. 4 (1983): 608–25; Carol A. Mullen, "Naturally Occurring Student-Faculty Mentoring Relationships: A Literature Review," in *The Blackwell Handbook of Mentoring: A Multiple Perspectives Approach*, ed. Tammy D. Allen and Lillian T. Eby (Malden, MA: Blackwell, 2007), 119–38; Johnson, *On Being a Mentor*, 97–103.

14. Malachowski, "The Mentoring Role," 92.

15. Johnson, *On Being a Mentor*, 98.

16. Ibid.

17. Daloz, *Mentor*, 215ff.

18. Johnson, *On Being a Mentor*, 99–100; Kram, "Phases of the Mentor Relationship," 616–17; Malachowski, "The Mentoring Role," 92.

19. Johnson, *On Being a Mentor*, 100–102.

20. Kram, "Phases of the Mentor Relationship," 609–10.

21. Diane M. Enerson, "Mentoring as Metaphor: An Opportunity for Innovation and Renewal," *New Directions for Teaching and Learning* 85 (2001): 11.

22. Astin, *What Matters in College?* 383.

23. Richard Light, "The Harvard Assessment Seminars: Second Report," *Explorations with Students and Faculty about Teaching, Learning, and Student Life* (1992): 32; Boyer, *Reinventing Undergraduate Education,* 15.

24. Daloz, *Mentor,* 245.

25. Johnson, *On Being a Mentor,* 11–13.

26. Marie A. Wunsch, "New Directions for Mentoring: An Organizational Development Perspective," *New Directions for Teaching and Learning* 57 (1994): 12; Malachowski, "The Mentoring Role," 105–106; Otto, "Mentoring," 18.

27. Johnson, *On Being a Mentor,* 12.

28. Janet L. Jones and Marcie M. Draheim, "Mutual Benefits: Undergraduate Assistance in Faculty Scholarship," *Journal on Excellence in College Teaching* 5, no. 2 (1994): 90–91.

29. Johnson, *On Being a Mentor,* 12; Malachowski, "The Mentoring Role," 105–6.

30. Otto, "Mentoring," 16–17; Marie A. Wunsch "Developing Mentoring Programs: Major Themes and Issues," *New Directions for Teaching and Learning* 57 (1994)" 30; Johnson, *On Being a Mentor,* 45–69.

31. Tim Elgren and Nancy Hensel, "Undergraduate Research Experiences: Synergies between Scholarship and Teaching," *Peer Review* 8, no. 1 (2006): 5; Johnson, *On Being a Mentor,* 13–20.

32. Wunsch, "Developing Mentoring Programs."

33. Maryann Jacobi, "Mentoring and Undergraduate Academic Success: A Literature Review," *Review of Educational Research* 6, no. 4 (Winter, 1991): 518. Jacobi reports that systematic studies on issues of gender and race in mentoring relationships have yet to be conducted. In particular, she notes the need for focused research on both the specific academic and developmental outcomes of these mentoring relationships (p. 520).

34. Margaret Scisney-Matlock and John Matlock, "Promoting Understanding of Diversity Through Mentoring Undergraduate Students," *New Directions for Teaching and Learning* 85 (2001): 80; Jacobi, "Mentoring and Undergraduate Academic Success," 511.

35. Johnson, *On Being a Mentor,* 99.

36. Ibid., 110.

37. Ibid.

38. Sheila Greeve Davaney, "Between Identity and Footnotes," in *Identity and the Politics of Scholarship in the Study of Religion,* ed. José Ignacio Cabezón and Sheila Greeve Davaney (New York: Routledge, 1994), 39.

39. Fernando F. Segovia, "And They Began to Speak in Other Tongues," in *Reading from This Place,* vol. 1, *Social Location and Biblical Interpretation in the United States,* ed. Fernando F. Segovia and Mary Ann Tolbert (Minneapolis: Fortress Press, 1995), 1–32; John R. Lanci, "To Teach Without a Net," in *Walk in the Ways of Wisdom,* ed. Shelly Matthews et al. (New York: Trinity Press International, 2003), 65–69.

40. Davaney, "Between Identity and Footnotes," 39.

4

Thinking about Method

Robin Rinehart

In the multidisciplinary realm of research in religious studies, questions of theory and method are absolutely crucial and almost always complex. Research in religious studies necessitates not only attention to theory and method but also an awareness of the researcher's own perspective and commitments and how they may affect the project. As a result, it is essential for mentors of Undergraduate Researchers in religious studies to assist their students in foregrounding these issues as they frame their research projects.

For many students, pursuing Undergraduate Research in religious studies may be the first opportunity they have had to design their own project from the ground up. For example, I teach at Lafayette College in Pennsylvania, a small, selective liberal arts/engineering school with a major in religious studies. I typically mentor students working on semester-long independent-study projects, semester-long capstone projects for the major, or two-semester honors thesis projects. Most frequently, the primary product of this research is a paper ranging from thirty or more pages for an independent study or capstone project to upwards of one hundred pages for an honors thesis. Students almost always tell me that these projects, which they typically conduct as seniors, are the first time they have ever written anything of that length.

Members of my department have agreed that one of our primary learning goals for students conducting capstone or honors thesis research is that students demonstrate an awareness of the theoretical issues that are relevant to their project and also demonstrate the ability to craft a methodological approach that is appropriate to the task. In this regard, the students' projects are often more complicated than the kind of research paper they may have written for other classes, which typically will have required library and other forms of research, but not necessarily an explicit methodological component.

Our religious studies majors have ideally already completed a course on theories of religion before they undertake capstone or honors thesis research. Determining whether or not students have completed such a course is an important first step in mentoring a research project. It is also important, however, to find out how much experience the student has had in applying theoretical models to data different than that illustrated in a model itself. A student may well be familiar with the definition of religion that anthropologist Clifford Geertz sets forth in his classic article "Religion as a Cultural System," for example, but still may not have had a chance to craft elements of this definition into a method to apply in his or her own research. Ideally, a course on theories of religion will not only address theories themselves, but also help students assess the relevance and applicability of given theories to different forms of religious expression and help them make the move of using a theory or theories to craft a method. It's also possible that a student may not have studied the kind of theories that best suits his or her topic. I have mentored students, for example, who are interested in issues related to gender and religion, but who have little prior background in theories of gender or the feminist critique of religion. There may also be students undertaking research in religious studies who have not had a course or other introduction to theory and method; they will need special guidance from their mentor in shaping the method they use for their project.

Paying explicit attention to theory and method in religious studies research typically will take the project to a level beyond that of the kinds of research papers and other assignments typical in undergraduate courses. As such, it's important for mentors to emphasize to students that their project is not just a means of exploring their own interests and fulfilling a requirement, but also represents a contribution to the larger ongoing conversations that take place throughout our field. For students who plan to pursue graduate work, such projects can be especially helpful in making the transition to graduate-level research.

Two of the four key criteria we have identified for Undergraduate Research in religious studies are particularly relevant to framing a methodological approach for a project (see chapter 1 for more detailed discussion of criteria of Undergraduate Research in religious studies). First, we define Undergraduate

Research as "selective" and most appropriate for students who are able to envision, sustain and complete a complex, high quality, and nuanced analysis. Second, we have explained that the Council on Undergraduate Research definition of Undergraduate Research as "an inquiry or investigation conducted by an undergraduate student that makes an original intellectual or creative contribution to the discipline"[1] can be understood in a variety of ways, such as encountering/uncovering new data which are incorporated into existing frameworks, discovering new insights or data that alter the boundaries and/or contours of the field, drawing novel comparisons or making heretofore unrecognized connections within the field, making new assessments of current knowledge/interpretations based on such standards, creating new visions or interpretive structures that re-integrate/reconfigure what is already known or accepted, applying existing interpretive structures in a new way or in new contexts in order to unfold distinctive integrations/configurations within the field.[2] Clearly the expectation of quality, nuanced analysis coupled with the types of contributions we envision an Undergraduate Researcher making requires attention to matters of method from the very beginning of the project when the student first shapes his or her research agenda.

Foregrounding Method in Framing the Project

> *I want to find out what dharma really means in Buddhism.*
> *I'm interested in how society perceives cults.*
> *I'm interested in women in the Catholic Church, or maybe women in the*
> *Roman Catholic Church compared to women in Protestant churches.*

Undergraduate students pursuing research projects in religious studies often begin with an idea that is too big to shape into a manageable research topic for a one-semester or year-long project, as the actual examples above show. I was the undergraduate who proposed the topic of "what dharma really means in Buddhism" many years ago; my professor told me it was a hopeless topic and that was that. I don't even remember what I chose to research instead; now, as a professor myself, I wonder how I would respond to a student who came to me with a similar proposed research topic and whether as an undergraduate someone might have guided me to develop a more focused and refined version of that question that interested me. Dissertation advisors often tell their Ph.D. students that they will end up writing a dissertation that is focused on about 10 percent of what they originally thought the dissertation would cover. If this is typical for graduate students, who have more experience in research and writing, and substantially more time for research and writing than a typical undergraduate, then what percentage of an original idea is likely to become the focus of an undergraduate project? How can faculty mentors preserve the enthusiasm and interest the student brings with the big idea but at the same time help the student develop a more manageable research question and develop appropriate methods for exploring that question?

In this chapter, I will address components of the process of framing methodological concerns in an Undergraduate Research project in religious studies. I begin with a series of very basic questions for the student and faculty mentor to explore concerning the proposed topic, the sources available on the topic, and the role of the student researcher's own perspective. Of course some of these preliminary factors may not be applicable or necessary in every case, depending on the experience the student brings to the project. I then turn to a discussion of common methodological perspectives used in the field of religious studies and how mentors may help students develop an effective, informed method for their projects.

Preliminary Considerations: Refining the Question, Reflecting on Perspective

It is essential that the faculty mentor encourage the student to begin the task of framing methodological considerations as part of the preliminary process of refining the research topic. The faculty mentor needs to discuss with the student her or his previous research experience in different fields and her or his grasp of methods from the field of religious studies as well and other humanities and social science disciplines that may be useful for the project (see chapter 10 for fuller discussion of this point). A student's work in other courses (e.g., an ethnography project in anthropology, an experiment in social psychology, a research paper in history) may be a useful starting point for conversation on how to frame a research question and identify the appropriate methods for pursuing it and for beginning to understand the complex terrain of shaping method. Given the multidisciplinary nature of religious studies research, the issue of method is central to framing any research project, and it is therefore important that the student and mentor talk about methodology as soon as the student begins to develop a specific research question.

In many science and some social science projects, for example in completing a laboratory experiment, it is typical for faculty to give guidelines about the research methods required. Many of the research assignments students complete in undergraduate humanities courses, too, may have included fairly specific instructions about the topics students may explore and the methods they may use to do so. Although data on Undergraduate Research and writing in the humanities are scarce, my own experience, as well as anecdotal evidence from colleagues at other institutions, suggests that many students, when they undertake a substantial research project in religious studies such as a honors thesis or senior capstone project, may not have had much experience with making substantive decisions on their own about the scope and method of a research project.

Even before turning to the questions of particular categories of research and the methods that may be applicable to a given project, ideally the faculty mentor should encourage students to explore basic questions about the specific nature of the question and how it might be framed, as well as encourage students to reflect on their own perspective. Let's return to one of the student project ideas from the opening of this chapter: *I'm interested in how society perceives cults.* What questions might the faculty mentor ask the student proposing this area of research? First of all, this idea requires clarification and definition of terms. Society—what society? American society? Is there a way to craft a more specific definition of the meaning of *society* intended here? Whose perceptions exactly, at what time? What data are available about such perceptions? How reliable are such data and what might their limitations be? How might you gather your own data, for example, by administering a survey or interviewing informants? Cults—how are you defining this term? To what extent are you aware of the substantial complications in defining a term that has both a specific technical definition in the history of religions as well as a popular, often pejorative usage? To explore this question, which specific "cults" do you wish to study? Answering such questions could be a useful first step in the student research project, with the faculty member recommending particular readings and other sources that can help the student focus the question more clearly.

Students whose knowledge of theory and method is limited may benefit from reading surveys that outline the history of religious studies theory and introduce the work of key theorists. Mentors may make recommendations based on the theories they think are most likely to be relevant for the student's research. There are a number of anthologies available, some highlighting famous theorists, others organized by method and discipline.[3]

As they read more widely in religious studies theory, students may be somewhat puzzled by the varying usages of the terms *theory*, *method*, and *methodology*, and the relations among them, in the context of religious studies and the sciences and popular discourse. In popular usage, *theory* often substitutes for "opinion," as in, "that's just your theory." In other contexts, particularly in the sciences, *theory* may refer to a set of well-established principles or rules.

Thus a scientist who refers to the "theory of evolution" may understand the term *theory* very differently from a creationist who dismisses evolution as "just a theory." In yet other contexts, the terms *theory* and *method* may be used interchangeably. Many religious studies texts use the terms *theory* and *method* without defining them clearly. There is also some confusion regarding the terms *method* and *methodology* and the relationship between the two. While *methodology* technically refers to the analysis of the methods used in a particular field, it is often used as what the *American Heritage Dictionary* (4th ed.) refers to as a "pretentious substitute" for method.[4] Whether intending to be pretentious or not, many religious studies scholars do use the term *methodology* when strictly speaking what they really mean is *method*.

Thus it may be helpful to point out to students that this variation in the usage of terminology is an issue, and to clarify what exactly we mean when we talk about theory and method in religious studies and how each of these concepts is important in framing a project. Bradley Herling defines theory as "a way of seeing something better in order to understand it, or looking beyond surface appearances to see the way something really is" and explains that theoretical ideas lead to better understanding through definition, description, explanation, and prediction.[5] Timothy Deal and William Beal suggest that "a theory is something like a conceptual lens, a pair of spectacles, that you use to frame and focus what you're looking at. It is a tool for discerning, deciphering, and making sense"; they add that "Religious Studies *is* theory; it is the myriad conceptual tools used to 'see' religion." Deal and Beal also point out that there is no "Grand Unifying Theory" in the academic study of religion: "every theory frames and focuses our attention on some things while leaving other things outside the frame or out of focus. Thus, religious studies is always in search of new theories that might open up new ways of seeing and interpreting religion."[6]

Carl Olson, distinguishing between theory and method, explains that a method is instrumental—it "performs a function that can be logical, conceptual, and logistical by bringing a subject into clearer focus, enabling one to construct paths of inquiry, and making analysis of one's findings possible."[7] Olson's discussion is useful for helping students understand the relationship between theory and method:

> A particular method is applied intentionally to the data being investigated, and it enables researchers to be systematic in their approach to the subject. Researchers establish methods to enable them to describe religious phenomena, to identify some phenomena as religious, to compare and contrast religious phenomena between

cultures, to approach subjects in a systematic way, to synthesize findings, and to critically analyze what one encounters and finds. A method can also help one construct an integrated and coherent theory. A theory is a construct from our experiences, encounters, and the application of methods. It enables us to unify our experiences into a coherent whole and to account for why something is the way that it is and not another way. By developing a theory, scholars argue for a particular position that they determine is valuable. Besides embodying positions and values, theories help us to construct an intellectual position from which we can argue for or against other theories.[8]

Herling, Deal and Beal, and Olson thus at least provide some guidance to students in thinking through the relationship between theory and method and how it will affect their project. It's worth noting that each of these authors uses terms such as *viewpoint, lens, frame, position,* further highlighting how important issues of perspective are in the study of religion.

Indeed yet another challenge for students as they begin their research, particularly as they read different types of source material, is figuring out how to characterize the perspective or theoretical stance of a particular author. In the case of scholarly literature, students may wish to characterize the theoretical perspective and methods employed, but this can be difficult if the work does not explicitly address matters of theory and method. Students may need some guidance in characterizing an author's approach, whether by discipline, insider/outsider status, critic/apologist, and so on. Sometimes this is as simple as reading the jacket blurb about the author ("John Smith is professor of cultural anthropology at...") or doing some Internet research on where the author teaches or was trained. We can also encourage students to look for specific references to different theories within a work, to pay close attention to the types of source materials a scholar uses, and to search for other clues regarding an author's methods.

Characterizing the perspective of an author can be especially daunting when the student is using nonscholarly sources because the specific perspective or even bias of the author in question may not immediately be clear. I have found that in early drafts of their research projects, students often cite different kinds of authors (e.g., scholars and critics) as authoritative sources of information without providing their readers hints as to the authors' backgrounds. As an example, a student researching women's roles in a specific religious tradition might cite Jane Jones, who says that the religion is irredeemably misogynist, and Jean Doe, who says that positive changes for women are taking place. It's important for students to recognize that their readers will want to know a bit more about Jones and Doe and what elements of their backgrounds may inform their positions. I've often told students that they have to act as detectives to identify how a particular authors' backgrounds and present positions may affect their perspectives.

Yet another step in this process of framing methodological concerns is reflecting on the perspective the researcher brings to her project. Let's use the second question from the beginning of the chapter: *I'm interested in women in the Catholic Church, or maybe women in the Roman Catholic Church compared to women in Protestant churches.* Here, the student and mentor need to talk about what personal interests and commitments may lie behind this question. Does the student come from a Roman Catholic or some sort of Protestant background? Does she have specific criticisms of the roles available to women in those traditions either historically or at present? Is she a critic of one branch of Christianity and an advocate for another? Is she an advocate for change in women's roles? Depending on the institutional context, religious studies programs are likely to have different views about the extent to which they encourage students to present or advocate particular theological perspectives and/or advocate specific change within a religious tradition. Even if the student's personal perspectives will not be highlighted in the final research product, it is essential for Undergraduate Researchers to think through these questions and how personal perspectives may affect their research strategies as they begin the project. Learning about the student's perspective may also help the faculty mentor make recommendations about particular theories of religion that may help shape the method the student uses. In the case of the student interested in women in the Catholic Church, feminist critical theory was obviously relevant, and reading in that area, in which scholars are typically quite explicit about their own commitments and agendas, helped the student think through and plan her own approach. Some students may find it helpful to read analyses of the insider/outsider issue in the study of religion for guidance on how they may clarify their own interpretive stance.[9]

A discussion of the student's perspective may be an appropriate moment for the mentor to discuss his or her own perspective as well. In my department, in which for many years I was the only female faculty member, I often mentored students who were interested in topics related to women's religious experiences. In some cases, this meant I took on projects that focused on religious traditions outside my own expertise in South Asian religions, such as the one that resulted from the questions I discussed above. Although mentoring a student in an area that isn't your own obviously presents some challenges and we may need to consult with other colleagues to provide the best advice to the student on sources, it also makes very clear to the student the conversational nature of our work and how their research doesn't just help them discover new knowledge, it helps others as well. It is a clear example of how we as faculty learn from our students.

The Next Step: Understanding the Nature of Sources

In addition to making a preliminary survey of the sources available, and reflecting on the role their own views will play in the research process, students need to identify and develop an awareness of the nature of the sources they will use. One way of framing this issue is to distinguish archival, textual, and ethnographic sources that will be useful for the project.

Using Archival Sources

Archival sources are those found in manuscript and document collections (see chapter 5 for more detailed discussion of student archival research). A student might choose to focus a project on an available archival collection that has not been studied in detail, such as a collection of papers from a local religious leader or organization. Such a project might be substantially devoted to cataloging, describing, and organizing the contents of the archive. Increasingly, many archives are available online. In the case of an archive that has already been documented and organized, the student may choose to analyze the choices that went into the selection and organization of a particular set of materials.[10] Analysis of the materials in a particular archive might also provide the basis for exploring a set of questions that interest the student; for example, a student interested in women's roles in a particular religious group might examine a set of women's letters, diaries, or other record.

As with most sources, issues of perspective and possible bias will be central to making use of such archival materials. The student working on "cults," for example, might consult an archive that preserves documents related to a particular group. As an example, there are numerous websites that make available documents related to David Koresh and the Branch Davidians. Some focus on the "anticult" perspective that views such groups as having implemented "mind control" techniques on their followers; others present differing views regarding the nature of affiliation with such groups and the processes that shape their development. Still others include documents related to the conflict between the Branch Davidians and governmental organizations such as the Bureau of Alcohol, Tobacco, and Firearms; the FBI; and the Justice Department.

A student working with archival sources will need to be aware as much as possible of the motivations behind the compilation of the archive, and also to ask what might be missing from it. Matters of method are central in developing the skills necessary to identify and develop a means of assessing the particular perspectives or biases of sources.

As I noted above, students need assistance and encouragement in developing the critical skills to identify different perspectives and how they may affect the selection and presentation of archival information, and they may be somewhat hesitant to characterize different perspectives in their written work. Perhaps some students think that by highlighting a particular author or source's possible biases they are challenging their authority; it's important for mentors to emphasize that when students highlight the perspective of a source, they are providing valuable information to their readers that helps them better understand the material.

Using Textual Sources

Textual sources are obviously at the heart of many religious studies research projects, and there are many ways religious texts can factor into a project (see chapter 9 for more detailed discussion of student projects working with texts). A specific text might itself be the focus of a project, for example, by analyzing how the text addresses a particular topic or by tracing how particular themes in the text have been interpreted in different contexts. A text or set of texts might also serve as the basis for a historical analysis of the representation of a particular event or ritual, theological point, or social issue. A variety of types of texts are available for undergraduate student research ranging from the sacred texts of various religious traditions to the primary sources of religious scholars and theologians to the official documents of various religious sects. For many undergraduate students who only think of sacred texts as the foundational documents of religious traditions, helping them expand their horizons to think about how other textual sources can serve as fertile ground for intellectual inquiry can help in the process of challenging students to think in new ways about how to ask questions within the discipline.

In developing a method for using texts in research, students will need to think through a number of central questions regarding textuality. They will need to be clear about and identify the nature of different religious texts, from primary sacred scriptures to oral "texts" to commentaries, differing interpretations of primary sacred texts, and so forth. Other important questions to consider include, what is the source of the text in question? Does the community which uses the text have a particular understanding of the authorship of the text? Are there multiple views on the origin of the text? Was the text composed in writing or orally? Did it initially circulate via oral transmission? If so, how did this affect the shape the text took over time? Are there multiple versions of the text? In what language(s) has the text circulated? The student researcher will need to consider issues of translation that may be relevant to the project. If using a text in translation, is there a generally accepted scholarly translation? Are there popular translations, and if so, do they differ from critical scholarly translations? Are there variant editions of the text in the original, and if so, to what extent do variant readings affect the question the student is considering? Recently, textual studies have also addressed the role of digitized resources.[11]

A text-based project could also incorporate a constructive component in its analysis. For example, the student researching women's roles in different branches of Christianity might consider foundational texts—including the Bible and denominational treatises—to see how they can be interpreted to reach different conclusions about issues such as women's ordination.

Using Ethnographic Sources

A student's research project may make use of already available ethnographic data, such as records of interviews of members of a particular religious tradition, and can also incorporate original ethnographic research (see chapter 7 for more detailed discussion of student projects that involve fieldwork). If the latter approach is pursued, the student may decide to design and conduct interviews or collect survey and questionnaire data. Participant observation can also be an important component of the project. A student researching women's roles in different Christian denominations, for example, might wish to visit representative church services and incorporate her own observations on how issues of gender are manifest in practice as a way of supplementing the self-reported attitudes about gender that are documented in interviews with religious leaders and community members.

Students incorporating ethnographic data in their projects will need to think about how to structure their collection of such data effectively. It is also crucial that they inform people whom they interview or survey how their responses will be used and ask permission to name and quote people as appropriate. Some types of interviewing and surveying may require the approval of the local Institutional Review Board; in such instances, it's critical for the faculty mentor to ensure that the student is aware of and complies with proper research protocol.[12]

In addition to the types of sources discussed above, some projects may involve the use of archeological evidence and other forms of material culture such as photographs, images, icons, or shrines. A student engaging such sources ideally will already have some background in the interpretation of iconography and other forms of religious art.

Framing Method

The types of sources the student decides to use in his or her project will necessitate particular questions about the perspectives and potential biases of different sources, whether they are archival, textual, or ethnographic. For example, the student exploring some aspect of societal perception of cults will need to be aware of the nature of the sources he or she uses and to develop a critical strategy for assessing sources that present an apologetic view, a critical view (both of which could serve as primary sources for the purposes of such a project), or some sort of scholarly assessment. The student exploring women's roles in Christianity will need to frame these issues in a slightly different way. What are the primary sources on which pronouncements regarding women's roles are based? How and by whom have those sources been interpreted? In this case, there may be primary biblical sources as well as later doctrinal pronouncements and commentarial traditions that serve as the "primary sources": there may be secondary sources that range from critical historical scholarly perspectives to theological endorsements or critiques.

As the student gathers and assesses different source materials for the project, a practical concern may arise. If there are many sources available, how can she or he determine which are most important? The student and faculty mentor will need to talk about how to choose representative examples relative to the length of time available for the project and the final form it will take. The student exploring perceptions of cults would need to decide which examples were most representative. The student exploring women's roles presumably will have identified a more specific focus for her research. For example, if she decided to focus on the role of women in two Protestant denominations in the last century, even then she most likely would have to select representative thinkers rather than attempt to survey all the views that have been put forth.

Thus far I have identified the first steps in developing a methodological approach for an Undergraduate Research project—defining the scope of a topic and critically assessing the nature of the available sources. With a clearly framed topic, the student then has decisions to make about what methods to adopt in interpreting and analyzing the sources.

One way to proceed is by thinking about method in very general categories. A student might choose to adopt a cultural studies approach, for example, as a way to interpret social constructions pertaining to individual and community identity and the sociopolitical forces that shape them. Or the student may select a historical studies approach in which he or she researches archeological and documentary sources to examine historical forces at work in shaping a particular event, figure, or movement. Other projects may be best served by a constructive or imaginative approach that draws together several different methods.

I recently worked with a student who was a double major in religious studies and sociology and was planning to pursue graduate work in sociology. For her religious studies capstone project, she wanted to explore representations of evil in American popular culture in the figure of the witch. During the early weeks of the semester, much of our conversation was devoted to the question of how exactly she would frame this project. Eventually, she ended up researching the Salem Witch Trials. In addition to reading scholarly works about the trials, she visited Salem and analyzed how witchcraft is represented there in the tourist culture of tours, museums, and pamphlets, and she also analyzed two television shows portraying witches, *Bewitched* and *Charmed*. Her project served as a good example of a constructive or imaginative method insofar as she combined historical research (Salem Witch Trials), ethnographic work (visiting Salem), and the study of popular culture, which included feminist critical theory regarding changing representations of women in America (*Bewitched* and *Charmed*). She also included a brief section on Arthur Miller's play *The Crucible* and the film of the same name as a means of illustrating how the example of the Salem Witch Trials, and the figure of the witch in general, has continued to serve as a means through which American society has explored perceptions of evil, enemies, the figure of the scapegoat, and constructions of gender and domesticity. Her project illustrates well how an Undergraduate Research project in religious studies can incorporate a range of different methods and address different types of theory.

As I've discussed in this chapter, faculty mentors need to help their students explore an important set of questions as they embark on a research project. What background in theory and method does the student bring to the project? What additional work might be necessary? What role does the student's own perspective play in shaping the final form the project will take? What are the appropriate sources to use, and what methods are best suited to those sources? By answering these questions as they pursue Undergraduate Research, students can experience directly the distinct challenges that arise in making choices about method and theory in the study of religion. Applying those methods to their own research shows students that they can make a meaningful contribution to the important conversations that take place in our field.

Student Reflection on Undergraduate Research as Integrative

Shelton Oakley

Reflecting on my four years of undergraduate education, the Undergraduate Research aspects of academia proved to be invaluable. Not only did research assignments require me to think more critically and thoroughly about the content at hand, but also these academic opportunities afforded me the unique freedom to explore further the topics of my personal selection and interest. By doing so, it created a space for me to hone and test my academic and vocational passions. In regards to my preparedness and decision to pursue graduate education, I still identify Undergraduate Research as one of the *most* beneficial and influential academic experiences...[M]y senior Undergraduate Research paper built upon former classroom discussion and curriculum, yet expanded what I knew as well as how I thought. No longer could I rely on the interpretation of certain texts and ideas germinated in the classroom; instead, I learned how to interpret people's perspectives as valuable and reliable research sources. Research opportunities such as these rendered me freedom and ownership in my work, thereby providing me the opportunity to practice critical thinking on a deeper level.

NOTES

1. See http://www.cur.org/about.html.
2. Working Statement on Undergraduate Research (see Appendix I).
3. William E. Deal and Timothy K. Beal, *Theory for Religious Studies* (New York: Routledge, 2004); Seth D. Kunin, *Theories of Religion: A Reader* (New Brunswick, N.J.: Rutgers University Press, 2006); Daniel L. Pals, *Eight Theories of Religion, 2nd ed.* (New York: Oxford University Press, 2006). Two recent works that specifically address the concerns of researchers beginning their work in Religious Studies are Carl Olson, *Theory and Method in the Study of Religion: A Selection of Critical Readings* (Belmont: Thomson/Wadsworth, 2003) and Bradley Herling, *A Beginner's Guide to the Study of Religion* (London: Continuum, 2007).
4. *The American Heritage® Dictionary of the English Language,* 4. s.v. "Methodology. http://dictionary.reference.com/browse/methodology (accessed June 12, 2009).
5. Herling, *A Beginner's Guide to the Study of Religion,* 24–25.
6. Deal and Beal, *Theory for Religious Studies,* xi.
7. Olson, *Theory and Method in the Study of Religion,* 9.
8. Ibid., 9–10.

9. Herling, *A Beginner's Guide to the Study of Religion,* 37–42, has a helpful discussion of this issue.

10. Barabara Heck, Elizabeth Preston, and Bill Svec, "A Survival Guide to Archival Research" is a good brief introduction to some of the practical matters involved in archival work, http://www.historians.org/perspectives/issues/2004/0412/0412arc1.cfm.

11. A useful introduction to current work in textual studies is Raimonda Modiano, Leroy F. Searle, and Peter Shillingsburg, eds. *Voice, Text, Hypertext : Emerging Practices in Textual Studies* (Seattle: University of Washington Press, 2004).

12. Students may wish to consult the 2004 American Anthropological Association's "Statement on Ethnography and Institutional Review Boards." http://www.aaanet.org/stmts/irb.htm.

PART II

Approaching Undergraduate Research in Religious Studies

As the chapters in the previous section demonstrate, Undergraduate Research can cultivate the development of research skills that enable undergraduate students to engage in theoretical and practical scholarship that opens their understanding of religion through new perspectives, angles of thought, and combinations of ideas. The chapters in this section demonstrate some of the ways faculty and students have made this possible through their participation in Undergraduate Research.

Undergraduate Research builds on the basic skills that are developed in religious studies departments and draws intentionally on the classroom experience of designing research and writing papers. Through exploration of a focused, discrete body of knowledge, developing a research agenda (e.g., a research question, methodology, research proposal), actively doing research, and developing a research product, Undergraduate Research requires an ability to manage time, set goals and deadlines, draft and refine a thesis, and revisit and revise research questions. Furthermore, it requires that students have a certain knowledge and skill base. This base necessarily entails connection to existing curricular goals and academic courses. Students should have a working understanding of some of the research methods of the discipline, as well as a willingness to apply methods in a constructive manner.

Whether the research topic is student or faculty generated, there are many research models for Undergraduate Research in religious studies. Some of the more common approaches are included in this section: archival (chapter 5), cultural studies (chapter 6), ethnographic (chapter 7), historical (chapter 8), and textual studies (chapter 9). Each approach is distinct and requires particular guidance and pedagogical and assessment strategies. As well, there are theoretical questions, skills and abilities, and types of research and writing associated with each model. Furthermore, these chapters illustrate well that Undergraduate Research occurs in many forms in our discipline, such as tutorials, directed inquiries, summer research fellowships, and student research assistantships, to name a few. In many cases, form is an outcome of institutional context, as related modes of assessment, guidelines, and opportunities for participation reflect a wide degree of standardization and support.

5

Exploring Archival Material

Paul O. Myhre

Introduction

Undergraduate Research projects pose daunting tasks for undergraduate students and faculty. First, students are generally not well acquainted with a range of methods required to do independent and original research in religious studies (for more discussion on methodology and student research see chaper 4). Most of a typical undergraduate's academic and research preparation and experience involves secondary research materials. Hence, a capacity to engage primary source documents and materials effectively requires systematic and structured teaching in order to provide the student with the tools required. The students' learning can be enhanced by providing them with a range of options and suggestions for how to take ownership for their own learning. This could include everything from design of the research project, discovery of what is required in order to effectively engage the research question(s), providing skills for concept mapping and preliminary charts of research accomplishments and missteps, and ongoing readjustment and development of the research project. This chapter will highlight some of the challenges and opportunities posed by Undergraduate Research involving archival methods. As a means toward assisting readers, a particular example of Undergraduate Research involving student archival work as a means toward original research will be provided throughout. It is hoped that this example will illustrate something of the complexity of archival research methods for undergraduate students, the potential for original insights, and the capacity for ongoing enthusiasm for a research project beyond the confines of a specific course.

Archival research could be regarded as an active pedagogical strategy by which students can work independently or in groups to gather materials that pertain to an overall research question. It is inherently self-generated and directed, yet it requires constant supervision and guidance. It is a method that requires a capacity to ask questions that might cluster around a central research question and to develop and ask additional questions that emerge directly from the research undertaken. It can even involve shifting the primary question to a secondary one in the face of particular evidence gathered through archival research. In the case of the Undergraduate Research project exemplar for this essay, the student was charged with the task of tracking down documents that might prove helpful for addressing or answering a fundamental research question about a particular Native American tribe's religious cosmology written in geological landforms.

The Undergraduate Research assignment was posed in general terms so as not to confine or limit the parameters of the student's research too swiftly. The student was charged with the task of correlating Early and Middle Mississippian period Native American geographical earthen mound locations in mound complexes with specific movements of the moon, sun, planets, and constellations in order to begin to develop theories about Mississippian cosmology. The student was also charged with the task of correlating visual artifacts from the period with alignments on the ground and in the sky. The thesis for the research was relatively simple: Early and Middle Mississippian mound complexes were aligned with the four cardinal directions, azimuth locations of the rising and setting sun during the winter and summer solstices, azimuth locations associated with an eighteen-plus-year cycle of full moons, azimuth locations of an eight-year cycle of Venus, annual cycles of specific constellations—particularly Redhorn (Orion)—and azimuth locations of the Milky Way galaxy during the summer solstice, winter solstice, and spring and fall equinox. Attention was also given to historic astronomical events: supernovae of 1006 and 1054 and the seventy-six-year cycle of Halley's comet. These alignments appear to have been directly tied to mound alignments, the annual cycle of ceremonies and rituals, and Mississippian cosmology. Archives represented one source of data for the Undergraduate Research project that could surface some of the details associated with specific artifacts and maps.

The project was immense and required an enormous amount of effort by both the student and myself as teacher/facilitator/mentor/coach for the research tasks to be accomplished in the course of one semester. At times the task seemed to be akin to peeling an onion. Every layer of observation required looking at an additional layer of evidence, making decisions about what to make of that evidence in relation to the previous evidence, and determining what the next steps of research would entail based on what had been discovered. Reading original documents was labor intensive in that I, as the professor, often had to secure the documents, provide guidance for how to interpret the materials, and help the student fit the relevant insights into an overall framework of learning. The student was also charged with locating primary research documents— maps and images, artifacts, and remnant tribal cosmological stories. It was a shared hope that these items could yield particular insights about Mississippian religious cosmology.

Since Mississippian culture flourished along the Ohio and Mississippi rivers and extended into regions within driving distance of Wabash College in Crawfordsville, Indiana, site visits were possible and archival materials located in both Indiana and Illinois were accessible to both teacher and student. Wabash College was ideally situated for this type of Undergraduate Research and served well as a hub for exploring this particularly complex research question. Hence, it seems imperative that Undergraduate Research archival projects require that faculty first take an inventory of the available archives within driving distance of the school so as to provide greater access for students to the relevant materials. Faculty familiarity with the resources can also aid in directing students toward specific materials that could address particular research questions that arise during the course of study.

Archival Research as Problem Based Learning

Michael R. Hill in his book *Archival Strategies and Techniques* provides helpful commentary for those interested in the prospect of archival work, particularly for those mentoring Undergraduate Research projects. He states, "My guiding understanding of archival work goes something like this: In archival work, what you find determines what you can analyze, and what you analyze struc-tures what you look for in archival collections. This is blatantly circular—and points to the necessarily provisional and iterative essence of ongoing archival work. Investigations in archives simply cannot be predicted or neatly packaged in methodological formulas that guarantee publishable results. That for me is an attraction, but to others it may seem too indeterminate, too risky."[1]

The predicted research methods required and results cannot be deter-mined in advance for archival research projects, and hence, learning goals and outcomes need to be drafted in a provisional and malleable framework. Part of the work faculty must do with students engaged with Undergraduate Research archival research projects involves constant monitoring of student learning needs and identification of potential growth areas for aiding student research skills development.[2]

Archival research requires an open mind for exploration of ideas, chasing insights gathered through investigation, and a willingness to continually reevaluate conclusions in the quest for understanding. Archival research can often seem tedious, and the amount of irrelevant evidence can sometimes outweigh the few pieces of relevant material. Students need to be made aware of this pitfall in advance of the work so that they will not be overly disappointed and dissuaded from the research.

Work with archival materials in the exemplar Undergraduate Research project for this essay required the student and me to engage in a process of investigation that involved a host of disciplines and areas of research. Each discipline required a degree of familiarity with methods appropriate to each. These included: astro-archeology, archeology, ethnographic studies, site observation, map reading and analysis, Native American tribal narratives, and Jesuit and other missionary narratives. In order for this type of Undergraduate Research to have any hope of success, the student would need to have had previous course work in religion, ethnography, archeology, or Native American religion or anthropology. Methods learned in the prerequisite Native American Religions course for the Undergraduate Research project and through other humanities-related undergraduate course work enabled the student to begin to read the primary and secondary source materials with greater sophistication than if no prerequisite had been required. Hence, archival research is not simply a matter of sifting through documents to discover a few particularly relevant ones. It is a process that requires continual assessment and reassessment of documents and persistent refinement of various research methods. It may even mean gaining proficiency in particular subfields in order to understand materials discovered, such as those associated with astro-archeology. With regard to astro-archeology methods, time restraints required that I as professor learn the requisite skills and then correlate and disseminate relevant information to the student. This proved to be a helpful strategy for expanding subsequent student interpretative skills in relation to artifacts and select tribal stories. Archival Undergraduate Research requires that the professor remain attentive to identifying and developing student skill sets required for the work. It also demands a keen eye toward that which may be beyond the capacity of the student during the course of the project. Sometimes this may require active involvement by the professor in the Undergraduate Research project itself.

Use of archival resources was an important part of the research. The archives on Native American history and culture are scattered across the United States, and access to them during the course of a semester can be a daunting task. The student visited archival sources in the region and visited archives that may hold additional materials for study in the St. Louis, Missouri, area following the end of the course term. His interest in the project continues to be fueled by preliminary work that had been accomplished over the course of one semester of study. In this case, one of the clear outcomes from Undergraduate Research has been a sustained level of interest in ongoing research and study.

Fortunately, with the rise of archival information available on the Internet, archival research has been streamlined somewhat and many documents that had been previously inaccessible are now available online. Access to many archival resources through the World Wide Web is relatively easy and less time consuming than prior modes of research that required a concentrated block of time for travel to collections located sometimes hundreds of miles from home. Although hands-on work with the documents themselves can be enlightening, current digital technology allows for closer examination of the documents than may be available to the naked eye in an archive. The fact that the documents are digitally available doesn't necessarily translate into how they might be researched by a student or how they might contribute to understanding a larger research question however. The process of archival research in religious studies always requires a degree of discernment for evaluating the quality of the materials themselves and a strong hermeneutical base for interpreting layers of meaning. Faculty will find that a significant portion of the work involving Undergraduate Research archival research in religious studies will involve developing student capacities for critical discernment of texts and artifacts in order for them to begin to make original contributions to the field.

A primary step in developing student capacity for Undergraduate Research archival work involves immersion in relevant secondary literature. Knowing what has been written about the topic, what research questions have been previously explored, and identifying particular lacuna related to a specific research question can aid in the work students will accomplish in archival investigation. In the example used here, the student's Undergraduate Research project required familiarity with secondary literature available on Mississippian culture and religious practice. The student read a host of secondary source documents and books in order to begin to understand the terrain over which the research would be conducted. The student was also encouraged to become familiar with anthropological, ethnographic, and archaeological research associated with antecedent mound-builder cultures—Adena and Hopewell—in order to compare and contrast the orientations of mound types and locations with that of Mississippian mound types and locations. The student was also required to read cultural stories associated with tribal groups that could be identified as possible remnant tribes: Illini, Shawnee, Cherokee, Chickasaw, Osage, and Caddo. Reading the tribal stories provided the student with a foundational appreciation for an array of religious and cultural stories, commonalities and differences, identification of hero figures and hero stories, development of sensitivity to Native American constructions of reality and religion, and so on. This background reading was crucial for establishing a foundation on which the scaffolding for student research and learning could be constructed. It also set the course for subsequent investigations of archival materials. Hence, any student who would embark on an Undergraduate Research project involving archival research ought to be informed that the work will require significantly more hours of reading, analysis, and writing than a typical undergraduate course in religious studies.

What might be regarded as archival methods? Can they be reduced to a particular set of methods, or do they require constant refinement and development in association with particular research questions? According to the *Blackwell's Companion to Organizations*, "In its most classic sense, archival methods are those that involve the study of historical documents; that is, documents created at some point in the relatively distant past, providing us access that we might not otherwise have to the organizations, individuals, and events of that earlier time."[3] Archival work may appear tedious and time consuming. Sifting through a mountain of materials may yield little that seems to contribute to the objective of the research. In this Undergraduate Research project the objective for the archival research was simple: locate and read Native American ethnographic documents, historical and research documents associated with Early and Middle Mississippian mound complex sites, analyze visual documentary records and maps of mound complex sites from the eighteenth and nineteenth centuries, and examine images and artifacts associated with Mississippian culture. The systematic examination of research data was tied routinely to the fundamental research question driving the Undergraduate Research project. Could discernment of specific correlations between Mississippian mound complex arrangements with astronomical movements of the sun, moon, and planets, correlated with artifacts and tribal stories, begin to provide insight into Mississippian religious cosmology?

For the Undergraduate Research project cited here, the student required an array of methods for engaging in the Undergraduate Research project. The work involved gaining a degree of proficiency with qualitative methods. These methods included—and were not limited to—observation, historic analysis, archival research, fieldwork, visual analysis, and human proportional analysis. The student needed to be fully immersed in the topic under study. This isn't an

easy task when undergraduate students are pulled by an array of other obligations—other course requirements and assignments, social and athletic involvement, and so on. Hence, it seems that the student has to exhibit an extremely
high level of interest in the topic in order for it to have any potential for making
an original contribution to the field of religious studies.

Adapting a method proposed by Artemus Ward for graduate students at
Northern Illinois University, I encouraged the Undergraduate Research student to read original documents and analyze the raw data. Ward's method
involved coding original documents for excerpts and themes, analyzing the
results, and drafting a summary analysis based on the data examined.[4] The
challenge for archival research is always one of sifting and selection. Deciding
which details to note and which ones to bypass is a constant part of the archival
research process.

Archival research involves handling primary source materials that have
not necessarily been interpreted by other researchers. It is a way by which to
gather and organize materials according to an artificial typology so that theories
about something might be tested or informed by the evidence. Archival materials are interrogated as they relate to the basic research question. Although it
can be subject to manipulation and misreading, it can also break open vistas of
insight into previously overlooked source materials. At its most rudimentary
level, archival resources are historic documents that provide written and visual
information about specific people, places, and events. In the case of this
particular Undergraduate Research project, there was an ongoing need to
examine early documents and sources for evidence that have since been lost or
reinterpreted. Much of the early missionary accounts provide insights about
remnant tribes that may have been related to the historic Mississippian people.
Since there are no historical records for the people who built the mound complex sites, reconstruction of the remnant tribal stories is an important step in
beginning to map Mississippian cosmology and mound alignments.

Developing Student Skills for Successful Archival Research

It is no secret that archival research can be deadly boring and provide students
with little stimulation for a given research project. However, if the student has
a specific task—to look for stories about Native American rites and rituals—
then the work can become something more. It may even take on the character
of a "treasure hunt" or "expedition" to an uncharted evidentiary terrain.

As mentioned previously, the student Undergraduate Research project
involved more than archival mining. It immersed the student in the murky

waters of documentary, geographical, and astronomical analysis. The student required contact with a host of methods in order to work toward some type of tangible conclusion for the semester. Although the work is ongoing over the summer and will recommence during the fall semester, college campuses run on a semester schedule and grades need to be assigned for work accomplished during a given term. Hence, one semester of work on an Undergraduate Research project of this type may not be sufficient to achieve an outcome that involves a contribution to original research. Yet, one semester is sufficient to expand the range of a student's capabilities with a range of research methods and to stimulate ongoing involvement with an Undergraduate Research project.

At least five archival research skills were determined to be key for the success of the Undergraduate Research project. First, the student needed to develop a degree of proficiency in reading maps created by early explorers and cartographers, maps that identified particular geographical locations and elevations associated with Mississippian mound-building culture, and maps associated with sky charts created by Native American tribes and pioneer astronomers. Second, the student needed to possess a degree of ability for mapping astronomical movements of planets, stars, the moon, and sun. This skill was needed when sifting through the documents so as not to miss some detail that may pertain to the alignments of earthen mounds. Third, the student required a degree of skill and cultivated imagination for reading Mississippian artifacts and images of those artifacts for clues that might indicate something about the particular alignments of the earthen structures. Fourth, the student needed to demonstrate an ability to effectively engage archaeological data and determine what might be relevant for the overall research question. Finally, the student needed an ability to engage historical documents at a variety of hermeneutical levels as he looked for clues about Mississippian mound alignments.

In my experience, archival research projects at the undergraduate level require students who are highly motivated and have previous academic experience with some of the methods required for addressing research questions. Additionally, students need to possess a capacity to learn new methods and apply what they have learned to the questions under consideration and to be able to work collaboratively with their professor as the research proceeds and is refined.

For example, map reading may seem at first to be a simple task. However, when reading historic maps, the task can become a bit more complicated. Cartographers in various periods of Native American history mapped landscapes of the Mississippian bottom differently. Some were aware of rivers and landforms, but not of the distances between them. Others were concerned with

charting strategic maps that would illustrate the density of indigenous populations in order to begin plans for their subsequent removal. Maps of the
Mississippian mound complex sites were varied in terms of distance and eleva-
tion of the various mounds. Mapmakers were also not always interested in
charting precise locations of Native American burial and platform mounds or
mound complex plazas and arrangement of mounds in the overall mound
complex. Instead, they were often concerned with agricultural aims. How
would the region be suited to farming practices?[5]

Undergraduate students involved with archival research can benefit greatly
from guided instruction by the professor. In particular, providing students with
a sharply focused topic for exploration in archival materials can assist them in
determining the processes for sifting through the mounds of material that will
be available to them.

A Collaborative Process

Faculty choosing to integrate Undergraduate Research into their own teaching
ought to first determine if they can commit a significant amount of time to
ongoing teaching preparation and increased student interaction sessions that
Undergraduate Research requires. In comparison to a standard three-hour
course, Undergraduate Research generally requires more time for preparation
and face-to-face student interaction. This is largely due to the malleable nature
of research projects and questions, student capabilities and learning needs, and
discoveries made through the research that may posit new questions and directions for investigation. That said, faculty hoping to use archival collections and
methodologies as a means toward introducing Undergraduate Research ought
to first inventory the availability of resources that could address potential
research questions. Second, faculty ought to clarify as much as possible the
scope of the project and provide the student with a degree of specificity about
the preliminary shape of the research question(s). Since many undergraduate
students may regard the idea of self-directed work that may eventuate in original
research as outside their capacity, it is important to discuss with them the scope
of the work envisioned and their potential capacity to accomplish it. In addition,
it is important to articulate clearly the research question(s) as you have envisioned it and establish specific ground rules for the collaborative work. This
can reduce misunderstanding later in the process of the research project. The
research question(s) also ought to be honed initially to something an undergraduate student might be able to undertake over the course of a semester or
school year. If the research question is too broad, the student will potentially be

flummoxed about how to narrow or refine it. If it is carefully articulated and agreed upon by both the student and faculty member, a research partnership is established. Once the partnership is founded, faculty are entrusted with the task of circling back regularly to the original question for review, refinement, and correction (for more discussion of the role of mentoring in Undergraduate Research, see chapter 3).

After the initial ground for Undergraduate Research collaboration has been laid, faculty ought to work with the student in developing an overall learning design for the Undergraduate Research project (for more detailed discussion of designing an Undergraduate Research project, see chapter 10). Crafting the scaffolding for the learning experience/Undergraduate Research project can go miles toward helping the student identify specific research goals, establish steps for the overall project that can help them meet those goals, build in ongoing assessment for checking progress, readjusting directions, or addressing confusing questions that the research may elicit, and provide faculty with ample opportunities to adjust or correct errant directions the research may suggest. In addition, students may exhibit a degree of timidity or be somewhat tentative about how to proceed with the work. I have found that it is important for a faculty member to consistently affirm student accomplishments, guide students when necessary toward specific methods or tools for analysis, and encourage them in partnership with you to design their own research parameters and questions. This can prompt a greater investment in the learning process by the student and aid faculty in their participation in the project. Regularly scheduled check-in sessions will aid the students in the process of refining their questions and research throughout the term. In ideal situations the Undergraduate Research project might extend over an entire school year for a particular student. In addition, if the Undergraduate Research project is such that more than one student could work either concurrently or in succession on a project, a momentum toward collaborative learning may eventuate that could extend beyond one year. Finally, when using archival materials it is important that faculty weave into the ongoing conversations specific tutorials about particular methods that may help students in their work with archival source documents.

Conclusion

Undergraduate Research projects that employ archival methods can produce significant results by advanced undergraduate students. The degree of student research interest in the topic can be enhanced through active learning methods that place the student directly in contact with primary course materials. Faculty will find that use of archives in service to Undergraduate Research projects requires a great degree of time and attention to the learning needs of the student involved with the research. It isn't uncommon for faculty to be pushed by the research questions as much as, if not more than, the student. Student success is also somewhat dependent on faculty participation in the active learning experience. Like any research project, archival work requires a capacity to change ideas in midstream as the data reviewed answers certain questions and raises others.

Undergraduate Research projects also require that a student both hold a capacity for learning complicated and diverse research methods and exhibit intellectual curiosity about the research topic and the promise of an original contribution to the field. As mentioned above, this project's research structure was designed largely around an inductive method or Problem Based Learning (PBL) approach that encouraged the student in partnership with me as faculty mentor/teacher to identify the areas of need in advance of the project and to identify those required as the needs would arise. Archival research set within a PBL framework can yield significant results.

In the case of the Undergraduate Research project highlighted throughout this essay, perhaps the greatest single outcome was not a contribution to original research, but the stimulation and development of a critically reflective undergraduate researcher. The skills the student acquired during one semester of work will provide solid footing for subsequent research projects in an array of subject areas. If student learning is the overarching goal for this project, then the project could be considered an unqualified success.

Student Reflection on Undergraduate Research

Brandon Cornett

The most interesting work I did involved my study of Native American culture. The things that I encountered while studying Native Americans were foreign to me. As I would discover, studying something completely new is exciting and provides an opportunity to engage an Undergraduate Research project without preconceived notions about what facets of the study might occupy the work. In our Undergraduate Research project, we started with the basics. Our study began with separating the idea of religion and worldview. This method enabled me to understand the foundations of a culture, paying attention to the details, while operating within a scope narrow enough not to be overwhelming. None of the classes I had taken before were taught like this, but it was something that I gladly applied to every course there after. Using the elements of Native American cosmology that I had learned in an introductory course to Native American religions I began my Undergraduate Research project on Mississippian cosmology. I knew that the Undergraduate Research project would be a lot of work since it involved trying to cover such a diverse grouping of cultures around the Mississippi river valley that were associated with Mississippian culture in 8th-12th centuries C.E. Not many other researchers have extensively explored Mississippian cosmology through geo-form alignments, archaeological artifacts, and remnant tribal stories. Every week that we met, we made progress on our research. Most of the things we investigated were new and exciting. We made connections and speculations that others had not yet published. The key to our successful research was always keeping the details in perspective.

NOTES

1. Michael R. Hill, *Archival Strategies and Techniques* (Thousand Oaks, CA: SAGE Publications, Inc., 1993), 8.

2. For additional information about research methods, see, The ERSC National Centre for Research Methods, http://www.ncrm.ac.uk/. It provides a good set of links to relevant research methods that could have some applicability for undergraduate students involved with religious studies research. For a good listing of links related to collaborative learning methods, see the Wabash Center's website Teaching Resources, http://www.wabashcenter.wabash.edu/resources/teach_all_result.aspx?keyword=colla borative+learning&fi lter=all (accessed March 15, 2011).

3. Marc J. Ventresca and John W. Mohr, "Archival Research Methods" in Joel A. Baum, ed., *The Blackwell Companion to Organizations* (Oxford, UK: Blackwell Publishers Ltd., 2005), 805.

4. Artemus Ward, "Qualitative Research Methods," http://polisci.niu.edu/ polisci/courses/fa07courses/545.htm (accessed March 9, 2011).

5. Contemporary maps provide more detail but lack specific site locations for some of the historic mounds. For example, Big Mound and mounds associated with it in St. Louis, Missouri, were utilized for fill dirt in the formation of the city during the mid-nineteenth century and were pilfered for Native American artifacts. Big Mound may have been the largest earthen mound ever constructed or at the least would have rivaled in size Monk's Mound at the Cahokia, Illinois mound complex site. This was one example of agricultural practices and city formational activities that prompted eradication of thousands of mounds over the past 150 years. Recent efforts by archaeologists using magnetometry (ground-penetrating radar) have provided evidence

for mound locations that had been previously removed or unrecorded. As more evidence becomes available it will provide researchers with a better grasp of the overall layout for a given mound complex site. The student involved with this Undergraduate Research project spent considerable time analyzing historic and contemporary maps that illustrated the design and layout of mound complex sites. For this Undergraduate Research project, various forms of engagement with maps and map reading have provided the student with a greater awareness of the need for precision in research projects—particularly those that involve precise alignments between mounds and astronomical movements of the sun, moon, planets, and stars.

6

Reading Religion and Culture

Carolyn M. Jones

In "Interdisciplinarity in Learning and Teaching in Religious Studies," Melanie J. Wright and Justin Meggitt, argue that religious studies has its roots in three traditions, in

> [t]he Orientalists' fascination with "the East," and
> *Religionwissenschaft*—the scientific study of religion as
> articulated in the nascent human sciences (anthropology,
> psychology, sociology). The third is the practice of
> comparative religion, by which students aimed to under-
> stand particular traditions, usually in relation to categories
> derived from their own dominant domestic religion
> (typically, Western Christianity).[1]

Religious studies, therefore, is an interdisciplinary activity, and a cultural studies approach to religious studies forefronts this interdisciplinary process as it engages in the readings of texts of various kinds: books, rituals, practices, and performances. In my area of the discipline, Arts, Literature, and Religion, reading as a professional is the skill that undergraduates must master. This reading, I want to argue here, is an ethical practice. Ethics and interdisciplinarity intersect in my work through the activity of practice. The idea of practice links ethics and interdisciplinarity to religion, both as a discipline and as a form of human expression.

   In terms of ethics, in one sense, as Jonathan Z. Smith reminds us, we "invent" the subjects we study.[2] Since religious studies is itself interdisciplinary, and my area completely so, issues of how to produce knowledge between disciplines are always at the forefront. In Undergraduate Research in cultural studies areas, the student, often, is working at the intersections of disciplines, moving across boundaries. This movement does not negate, in any way, a discipline's integrity, though it may question its assumptions. Therefore, knowing the methods, content, and consequent boundaries of disciplines and respecting them becomes a key element of learning. Interdisciplinary cultural studies work demands, therefore, that we call on a large "tool kit," to understand the texts we address. Wendy Doniger reminds us that we must be careful of how we deploy categories of similarity and difference as we work, avoiding "paralyzing reductionism and demeaning essentialism."[3] She argues in *The Implied Spider: Politics and Theology in Myth*: "Surely it is possible to bring into a single (if not necessarily harmonious) conversation the genuinely different approaches that several cultures have made to similar (if not the same) human problems."[4] Then, the "text you look at becomes a text you look through; the mirror becomes a window."[5] Helping students to look through windows, to do analytical work, rather than look at themselves in mirrors, to see either the self or one method everywhere, is one important task in interdisciplinary work.

Such practice builds skills. As parents, legislatures, and employers call for accountability in assessing what students can do, Undergraduate Research assumes a more prominent role in cultural studies. Employers, as Wright and Meggitt, rightly suggest, are forcing us to move the emphasis from "older configurations of knowledge...to transferable skills and competencies" (the shift from "what do students understand?" to "what can they do?")[6] The task of Undergraduate Research in cultural studies is to show how such work is "doing." We might, as Charles H. Long put it in a lecture at Drew University, suggest that the "doing"—the action such Undergraduate Research generates—is significant. "The importance of thought," Long said, "is not action. It is the creation of a form of meaning that affirms a community's meaning [and] identity."[7] And, I would add, the importance of thought is that it helps the individual understand and envision his or her role in that community and how he or she shares that identity. This is the kind of Undergraduate Research in which many of my students engage. Here, I want to look at two elements of that Undergraduate Research: reading as a professional and interdisciplinary research.

Undergraduate Research at the University of Georgia takes several forms. Some students in the Honors College choose to write a thesis of about thirty-five pages. This thesis is similar to a master's thesis in that the student must defend it before his or her director and another reader, create a PDF of the paper, and post it to the library collections. Some of these papers, or parts of them, will be presented at the CURO (Center for Undergraduate Research Opportunities) conference for Undergraduate Research. Young scholars come from all over Georgia and, indeed, the United States, to present research at that conference. Other students write an essay to enter in the undergraduate paper competition (sometimes this is in conjunction with CURO, sometimes not). Still others engage in an independent study to explore some dimension of the field that they cannot explore in a class. Regardless of the form, all of the students I work with are developing certain skills.

Undergraduate Research involves the idea, as the University of Georgia's CURO website says, of promoting "opportunities for undergraduate students to engage in research with premier research faculty." At UGA, we accept the "premise that it is possible for undergraduate students and faculty members to cooperatively engage in the creation of knowledge" as "partners in a learning community" and in "mentoring relationships" focused on conducting research.[8]

Participating in Undergraduate Research involves the whole student and contributes to "the intellectual, professional, and personal growth of the student." Undergraduate Research also develops the kinds of skills that potential employers value. Students learn the skills necessary to:

- identify and develop research topics
- formulate concise questions
- anticipate and think through problems and generate solutions
- develop frameworks to accomplish goals
- work collaboratively toward a common goal
- communicate effectively using the written and spoken word
- think critically
- evaluate objectively
- present and share knowledge effectively.[9]

Two challenges arise in developing these skills for students undertaking cultural studies research: reading as a professional and tackling an interdisciplinary project, which entails a particular kind of reading. John Guillory, in "The Ethical Practice of Modernity," has unpacked what professional reading— that is to say, reading as a researcher—involves. Working with Michel Foucault's final work in the third volume of *The History of Sexuality*, *The Care of the Self*, Guillory argues that reading is an ethical practice. It involves a form of self-improvement. In reading as professionals, however, we move beyond self-improvement for its own sake and toward Foucault's sense of "care of self" as connected to community—that is, reading for the good of others, not just for isolated pleasure. Reading, therefore, involves a choice among and between goods; it is engaged in particular "domains of action."[10] Framing reading in this way, Guillory uses Foucault to break reading out from a modern, individualist practice to situate it in a network of relations. For the professional reader, reading is not a private, but a public act, and one that requires reflection. Guillory, therefore, argues that professional reading and "lay" reading differ in their activity. Let me set out Guillory's argument.

First, professional reading is a form of work, and as work it demands time and resources, and it is compensated. Lay reading, in contrast, is a form of leisure. Though a professional reader and a lay reader may read the same work, each reads it in a different way.

Second, professional reading is a disciplinary activity. As such, it is "governed by conventions of interpretation and protocols of research developed over many decades."[11] What is important for Undergraduate Research here is to recognize that this kind of reading is something one *masters* over a period of years and is something that has structure. The degrees we grant signify this mastery. This is the most difficult dimension of cultural studies research, helping students see and respect disciplinary integrity. Lay reading, in contrast, has different conventions. One might examine, for example, when a lay reader reads (late at night, on weekends, when on vacation) and what that reader reads (magazines, newspapers, fiction, self-help books) to contrast with the work of the professional reader.

Third, professional reading requires vigilance:

> [I]t stands back from the experience of pleasure in reading, not in order to cancel out this pleasure, but in order necessarily to be wary of it, so that the experience of reading does not begin and end in the pleasure of consumption, but gives rise to a certain sustained reflection.[12]

Lay reading is motivated by pleasure, not vigilance. A lay reader reads for fun.

Finally, professional reading is a communal practice. The work is done in private, but the act of reading is connected to a variety of demands and audiences. For example, by reading, professional readers move toward publication, presentation, and teaching. All these venues open the reader's work to professional judgment, while lay reading, in contrast, is a solitary practice.[13] It is not engaged in formal settings.

What Guillory proposes—and what I move Undergraduate Researchers to do—is to dislocate reading from the aesthetic realm ("I like it because it moves me or is pretty") and what Guillory suggests is a moral realm[14] ("I am improved when I read this") and into the realm of ethics: doing. In doing, one applies directly to how to live, and the action of reading can be judged.[15] We academics engage in this practice of judgment of one another's work in publication, in giving academic papers, and in talking with colleagues. Our work is open to discussion and correction. This is what builds knowledge.

Guillory's ideas intersect with religious studies work in cultural studies. Many students who work with me are researching an area—whether a text or an idea—about which they care deeply. Their topics are personal as well as academic, questions about the complex world in which they live. I ask them to see that their work may begin as a private or personal question, but it has implications for the world they live in; this is the first step to reading as a professional. I also suggest that they might present the work, either send it out for publication or present it in CURO or at some other conference. For students in religion, reading and reflection in this new sense is linked to practice. Craig Dysktra, in "Reconceiving Practice," argues that "[o]ne person's action becomes practice only insofar as it is participation in the larger community and a tradition."[16] For Dykstra, "A practice is a sustained, cooperative, pattern of human activity that is big enough, rich enough, and complex enough to address some fundamental feature of human existence."[17] This resonates with Foucault's insistence that the value of any activity rests in its contribution to *a holistic framework of meaning* in someone's life. It is not limited to the good of a particular action: rather the action finds its good in itself and even more so, in its fitting into a larger moral, teleological framework.

For me, the pleasure inherent in lay reading is the lure to getting students to begin the practice of reading as professionals. Most of my students work with literature, generally modern literature. They, in traditional Religion and Literature research, are looking for religious patterns, subjects, and displacements in the secular arts. I have directed undergraduate research on the Beats, on Modernist Poetry, Yeats and Eliot, on popular fiction writers like Anne Rice, and on theory from Otto and Eliade to Derrida. One way that I have introduced students to the practice of reading—which we do at a slower pace than pleasure reading—is the reading journal. Students may work with the journal in different ways. Some compose on the computer; others buy a bound book of some kind, which I prefer, and within it, track their reading. The student is working between text, which she or he annotates, and journal, in which she or he questions and reflects. Writing by hand, in the margins and in the journal, slows the student down and helps generate an intimacy with the material that the computer technology that drives much of their daily lives does not. Their first step in the research process is private and therefore familiar to them as lay readers.

However, rather than simply reading for pleasure, they must now take notes, highlight particular passages, reflect on what they have read, and construct questions to bring to our meetings. These new elements of critical awareness about the text begin to move the student toward thinking and practicing as a professional reader.

Students like to do this kind of reading for several reasons. Most students are indoctrinated into the production of a product in their undergraduate education. This is a consumer model and does not work in research, which may produce a paper or book but is an ongoing inquiry. The reading journal model takes away the stress of having to come up with a topic right away, and it lets them ask the "dumb questions" they are generally either afraid or do not have time to ask if they think they need to start writing formally immediately. And finally, most of them have never had this kind of experience of reading in college. The process moves them as readers toward a professional space and complicates in a necessary and intentional way their notions of leisure and pleasure, work and public.

Two things happen when we slow the pace down. Students begin to dig into texts and to discover and work in their own rhythms. This allows the students to unpack complex arguments, to learn to appreciate an author's style, with all its nuances, and to follow both carefully. They see, to carry Guillory's use of Foucault forward, that the text is produced, with all the implications of that term, and that they, in writing about it, are producing a further signification. They see how scholars can do violence to one another's disciplines, subsuming another discipline's governing methods and approaches into their own without knowing its boundaries. I would argue that religion as a discipline faces this all the time.

Students, then, recognize that they require a method or theory (or more than one) to read the text from a particular angle, their own, and they begin to search for the tool they need—whether postmodern theory, new critical close reading, or some combination of methods. In my students' work, a sound, better-documented and better-argued *thesis* emerges from this kind of reading rather than their making a decision on a *topic* and reading toward that topic, which generally ends in summarizing material without any angle of argument.

This ties their work to disciplinary integrity. One important element of disciplines is the methods that they employ. Religious studies is interdisciplinary, drawing from sociology, anthropology, postmodern theory, and so on. To be cognizant of what these methods demand means that a student shapes a thesis and approaches it with intent. Many papers, even thesis papers, can be summaries of readings, without any critical perspective. This "book report" mode is what I consider a topic: it simply relates information. A thesis is argued. It may engage the same readings, but it takes an analytical perspective and uses a method to organize the material in a new way.

Julie Thompson Klein, one of the foremost scholars of interdisciplinary work, points out, in her definition of *interdisciplinarity*, that no one is sure what interdisciplinarity really is:

> Interdisciplinarity has been variously defined in this century: as a methodology, a concept, a process, a way of thinking, a philosophy, and a reflexive ideology. It has been linked with attempts to expose the dangers of fragmentation, reestablish old connections, to explore emerging relations, and to create new subjects adequate to handle our practical and conceptual needs. Cutting across all these theories is one recurring idea. Interdisciplinarity is a means of solving problems and answering questions that cannot be satisfactorily addressed using single methods or approaches. Whether the context is short-range instrumentality or a long-range reconceptualization of epistemology, the concept represents an important attempt to define and establish common ground.[18]

I would argue that interdisciplinarity might, in one form of one's work or another, involve all or some of the issues Klein lists. Interdisciplinary work is demanding, hence our work in religious studies is demanding. Both call for the integration of "data, methods, tools, concepts, and theories" of more than one discipline "in order to create a holistic view or common understanding of a complex issue, question, or problem."[19]

Successful interdisciplinary work is defined in various ways. Some scholars argue that it must interrogate the status quo, generating an intensive intersection between disciplines. Others, like Richard Carp, argue that interdisciplinary work is "bridge-building"; while others suggest that "restructuring" in interdisciplinary work changes each discipline involved.[20] One such interdisciplinary model in religious studies is womanist scholarship's taking narrative fiction as "data" for ethical reflection. When Katie G. Cannon, for example, in *Black Womanist Ethics*, used Zora Neale Hurston's work as a model for ethics, boundaries shifted and horizons opened in religious studies. A similar shift occurred when Toni Morrison's *Beloved* was published. Morrison's use of a historical case to create a work of fiction placed her on a variety of borders. That novel was one I saw taught in a variety of disciplines, from English to psychology to religious studies. The novel opened up discussion across disciplines, as it was, for literature, a Pulitzer Prize–winning novel, a neoslave narrative with a postmodern slant; for psychology, an exploration of the psyche of the slave; and for religion, an exploration of the ways that people under oppression made meaning.

Paulo Freire and Ira Shor's *A Pedagogy for Liberation: Dialogues on Transforming Education* describes the issues that professional reading and interdisciplinary work bring forward. First, this work can generate fear: the critical challenge that transformative pedagogies, like interdisciplinary work, sets out is scary. Second, it challenges hierarchy but more important, it challenges consciousness by bringing into light what is often denied and hidden in the myths we live by. These issues of power come to the fore. Finally, Freire says that transformative pedagogies can hold contradiction—and this is hard for people. "Human action," he tells Shor, can move in several directions at once: "something can contain itself and its opposite also."[21] This is difficult to grasp, much less to accept, yet, it stands at the core of ethics.

Cultural studies as interdisciplinary work and professional reading clarifies choices: it puts before us the issues at risk. This forces us to put ourselves into relationship between individual experience and the larger moment[22] and brings forward questions of what education is *for*. Are we teaching skills, or are we involved in some larger project? Such research responds to the concerns of the larger world that watches the university.

In doing such research, we *do* gain self-improvement. I think that such research, thereby, responds to the individual needs of the students. They also find themselves addressing larger, cultural needs. In working with literature, my students and I tend to engage in looking at "high," "folk," and "popular" culture. High-culture texts, like William Blake's poems and prints, have had an influence on current popular music, for example, on the Smashing Pumpkins who both perform and explain work on their website.[23] Such intertextuality and displacement of "high" culture into popular and folk culture illustrates the borders my students explore and on which we all reside.

Undergraduate Research in culture is mutually beneficial, to my students and me. I think and write about identity as fluid, performed, and nonessential. My students live in a world in which that is part of their everyday lives, as they perform the self on Facebook and MySpace and on their blogs. I think and write about language, meaning, and signification. They use Twitter and text. I think and write about—and live in—traditional communities of academy and church. I think about hybridity within tradition. They, often, live outside these communities or on their borders and they are making the hybrids, that is, "making religion" in ways that are creative and transgressive. I was prepared to teach in a secular world. They live in that world and, in their meaning making, blur the boundaries between secular and sacred by finding meaning in being tattooed or in popular music from Tupac to the Pumpkins.

Indeed, there are issues to explore on both sides, theirs and mine. Like Charles Taylor, in the *Ethics of Authenticity*, I worry about the radical, stylized, constantly performed self.[24] My students assert that they see little difference between the radically individual self and being a self for others. I have a deep sense of the distances between public and private spaces and, as an African American, the need for masks; they merge the realms, show their faces, but are surprised when that becomes problematic. In short, there is something in the tradition that they need. It is theirs, but they rarely know that or claim it, and I give them what I know of it in our work on literature, theory, and culture. *Canon* means measure or rule, and the students seek something against which to measure their ideas. We play across the border between their creativity and the rules and measures set up by professional reading.

The Element of Transformation

Students, even those engaged in Undergraduate Research, are sometimes hesitant to embrace ambiguity, to let contradiction stand. This hesitation can be soothed by a sound relationship with the research advisor and by the practice of using a journal that I have described above. This practice can be used by almost anyone, either in classes or in Undergraduate Research. Students, as my colleague Reid Lockin, one of the editors of the *Spotlight on Teaching*, put it, "lose control" of difficult texts.[25] To demonstrate and to employ this form of reading offers an entry into texts as the microcosm—the passage, paragraph, or even phrase—illuminates the macrocosm—the chapter or text. Such reading also prepares the space for fruitful discussion between director and student.

The question for any pedagogical practice is why do it and how to do it. We have examined the "why?" as teachers, but students need to consider the "why?" as they determine whether they want to engage in Undergraduate Research. What is the aim? What will it offer them that the classroom experience cannot? What do they desire the outcome to be? The "how" is the practice. As the student and I determine what texts she or he wants to read— usually two to four texts in a semester—I begin to identify the significant passages and themes on which I want the student to concentrate. After a first discussion of reading, I determine whether the student needs this kind of journaling guidance. If so, I ask the student, for the next meeting, to focus on a particular passage of the text, to journal about it (both what it says and what she thinks it means), and why it is important. In the next meeting, we start with that passage. This lets me track student reading and make any adjustments. Perhaps, the next time, we will concentrate on a paragraph, not a passage. Such a practice makes the most of the student's and my time.

Whether in Undergraduate Research or in a class, students, in their assessment of the work we have done, always comment that they probably would have read texts differently without this practice. They admit that they would have overlooked significant passages. For me, this is teaching skills and, at the same time, teaching for transformation.

If transformation is to change students into lifelong learners, this skill of reading and reflection gives them "rules," a way of doing things, that lead to an understanding on which, if they want, they can signify and improvise. For me, this is not just knowledge, but freedom—and both move beyond the boundaries of the classroom.

Conclusion

Guillory bemoans the loss of a productive space between lay and professional reading.[26] Undergraduate Research—indeed, all the teaching we do—may take place in that space. The productive space may just be relationship, the mentoring relationship between professor and student. Foucault argues that effective care of self, through physical activity, meditation, and intellectual activity, requires a network of others. One is always reading the works of others, educating one's self. One has conversations with friends: with both confidants and, more important, with a "master" figure who acts as spiritual director and guide; and one is engaged in correspondence "in which one reveals the state of one's soul, solicits advice, [and] gives advice to anyone who needs it."[27] Far from an activity that isolates the human being, therefore, self-care becomes a movement toward the world, "a true social practice" and "an intensification of social relations" that transforms the self and the other.[28] This is a good description of Undergraduate Research as well, as it engages the whole student. In entering research, the student steps onto a terrain that is both mapped and contested. On the journey, the student learns the map, and, in remapping, steps off its edge, into the world to make a change.

Student Reflection on Collaborative Inquiry

Lindsey Hammond

The exchange between our team and the individuals we interviewed lies at the center of our collaborative project. This exchange was the core from which ideas, questions, methodologies, and insights emerged and fruitfully developed. Our focus changed and evolved as we reached negative conclusions and generated new hypotheses to test. However, through this process I experienced the fulfillment of creating original ideas and research as we recorded our findings...The practice of formulating good questions and, therefore, making "original intellectual or creative contributions" to the discipline of Religious Studies and places where I have worked has been extremely rewarding. After graduation this experience helped me demonstrate to prospective employers the important skill sets that I had honed in my undergraduate studies, which culminated in this collaborative project, such as critical thinking and analytical skills, written and verbal communication skills, as well as self-starting and self-directed work habits while also being able to work as a team member. Not only have I gained specific skills as a result of being a part of this collaborative Undergraduate Research project, I have also benefited from being better prepared to meaningfully advance the work of the academy and the church.

NOTES

1. Melanie J. Wright and Justin Meggitt, "Interdisciplinarity in Learning and Teaching in Religious Studies," in *Interdisciplinary Learning and Teaching in Higher Education: Theory and Practice*, edited by Balasubramanyam Chandramohan and Stephen Fallows (New York: Routledge, 2009), 153.

2. Jonathan Z. Smith, "Religion and Religious Studies: No Difference at All," *Soundings* 71 (1988): 231–44.

3. Wendy Doniger, "From *The Implied Spider: Politics and Theology in Myth*," in *Theory and Method in the Study of Religion: A Selection of Critical Readings*, edited by Carl Olson (Belmont, CA: Thompson Wadsworth, 2003), 198.

4. Ibid., 200.

5. Ibid., 199.

6. Wright and Meggitt, "Interdisciplinarity in Learning," 153.

7. Charles H. Long, "God-Talk with Black Thinkers," Drew University, September 27, 2008.

8. University of Georgia, "CURO Center and Undergraduate Research Opportunities," http://www.uga.edu/honors/curo/about/index.html (accessed August 31, 2009).

9. Ibid.

10. John Guillory, "The Ethical Practice of Modernity: The Example of Reading," in *The Turn to Ethics*, edited by Marjorie Garber, Beatrice Hanssen, and Rebecca L. Walkowitz (New York: Routledge, 2000), 36, 38.

11. Ibid., 31.

12. Ibid.

13. Ibid., 32.

14. Ibid., 36.

15. Ibid., 38.

16. Craig Dystra, "Reconceiving Practice," in *Shifting Boundaries: Contextual Approaches to the Structure of Theological Education*, edited by Barbara G. Wheeler and Edward Farley (Louisville, KY: Westminster/John Knox Press, 1991), 37.

17. Charles R. Foster, Lisa Dahill, Larry Golemon, and Barbara Wang Tolentino, *Educating Clergy: Teaching Practices and Pastoral Imagination* (San Francisco: Jossey-Bass, 2005), 27.

18. Julie Thompson Klein, *Interdisciplinarity: History, Theory and Practice* (Detroit: Wayne State University Press, 1990), 196.

19. Ibid., 55.

20. Ibid., 27.

21. Paulo Freire and Ira Shore, *A Pedagogy for Liberation: Dialogues on Transforming Education* (Massachusetts: Bergin and Garvey, 1987), 69.

22. Ibid., 63.

23. Adam Ware, *Speaking in Rhyme and Riddle: Hybridity in Billy Corgan's Machina*. MA Thesis, University of Georgia, Religion Department, 2007.

24. Charles Taylor, *The Ethics of Authenticity* (Boston: Harvard University Press, 1992).

25. Conversation, May 18, 2010.

26. Guillory, 45–46.

27. Michel Foucault, *The History of Sexuality*, trans. Robert Hurley (New York: Vintage Press, 1988), 3:51.

28. Ibid, 3:53.

7

Sending Students into the Field

Jeffrey M. Brackett

Ethnographic Possibilities for Undergraduate Research

The range and flexibility of ethnographic research methods make it especially appealing as a model for Undergraduate Research in religious studies. In this chapter I will focus primarily on the work of one of my students, Nevada, who conducted a three-semester long ethnographic study of a Burmese Theravada Buddhist community in Fort Wayne, Indiana. Her work demonstrates how ethnographic research methods can work especially well when done for a sustained period of time. I intersperse her reflections on becoming an ethnographer, as well as my own reflections on the mentoring and teaching processes, in order to enable readers to see one possible way of using an ethnographic model for Undergraduate Research. Nevada's work illustrates a range of issues that arise in teaching ethnography, shows the polymethodic, transdisciplinary nature of religious studies, and fits well with pedagogical goals that are process-oriented with regard to learning outcomes.

While no definition captures the complexities or range of modern ethnographic methods, theories, or debates, I include the following definition as basic background for this chapter, which emphasizes the importance of fieldwork. Karen O'Reilly writes:

Minimally ethnography is

- iterative-inductive research (that evolves in design through the study), drawing on
- a family of methods,
- involving direct and sustained contact with human agents
- within the context of their daily lives (and cultures);
- watching what happens, listening to what is said, asking questions, and
- producing a richly written account
- that respects the irreducibility of human experience,
- that acknowledges the role of theory
- as well as the researcher's own role,
- and that views humans as part object/part subject[1]

Which particular aspects of ethnographic research one wishes to emphasize varies widely, as one might expect. In my teaching of ethnography, I especially emphasize self-reflexivity in student writing. The example I use in this chapter regularly illustrates varying degrees of self-reflexivity.

Institutional Location for Ethnographic Studies

My training is in religious studies, with a focus on popular Hindu practice in contemporary India, where I lived for three consecutive years (1996–99) conducting fieldwork and intensive language study. Apart from ethnographic methods, my interest is in locating "religion" within everyday life, especially outside of religious institutions. Teaching ethnography as Undergraduate Research allows me to challenge students' taken-for-granted assumptions about "religion" by getting them out of the classroom to observe (and sometimes participate in) religion as practiced inside and outside of institutional settings.

At Ball State University I teach in a joint department of philosophy and religious studies. BSU is a comprehensive university that regularly has approximately 16,000 undergraduate students, and another 4,000 graduate students. We do not offer a graduate degree in religious studies, but graduate students in cultural anthropology have enrolled in my seminar or have invited me to be one of their graduate committee members. Beginning in the academic year 2008–09 we implemented a new religious studies curriculum, with a thematic focus on "religion in culture." That same year our tenure-lines doubled from two to four, which greatly benefits students, faculty, our program, and the university generally. With increased impetus on campus toward engaged learning that incorporates immersive learning opportunities, a course in ethnography of religion is a win-win situation. Participant observation methods may not precisely align with immersive learning in the strictest sense, but it offers students a good deal of learning opportunities outside of the classroom. Since I prefer to teach religion from the "lived religion" perspective noted above, I am able to meet both programmatic and broader curricular demands. At this point we do not have either a method and theory course or a capstone seminar in our program. That may change, of course. However, this situation justifies teaching theory and method in every course to a certain degree and raising the emphasis on theory and critical issues in our 400-level courses such as my Ethnography of Religion course.[2]

Classroom Setting as an Entrée into Undergraduate Research

The majority of students who enroll in my "Ethnography of Religion" seminar do so only for one semester, thereby seriously limiting their opportunities for making a unique contribution to the field of religious studies. Although I will go into greater detail about one student's Undergraduate Research project, I will briefly mention ways in which Undergraduate Research may occur—or at least prepare students for Undergraduate Research—in a classroom setting. Since this course falls under the rubric of a "variable content" course, students have the option of taking the course a second time (pending instructor approval). Nevada began her project in a spring semester, followed it up in greater detail when I taught the same—but radically revised—course the next fall term, and then reoriented her work as an Independent Study with me in the spring semester. Overall, then, she had more than an entire year to develop her ethnography. The paper written for the Independent Study was then presented at our regional AAR meeting later in the semester. Although she submitted it as an undergraduate paper, the organizers placed her on a panel on which she was the only undergraduate. Her sustained attention to her ethnographic project better reflected the learning goals of Undergraduate Research than a single-semester course. However, I argue that even that semester-long course can result in a unique contribution to the field. It all depends on how one defines that "unique contribution." The unique contribution to the field made by this "sample" student is directly tied to the opportunities afforded her by being a student at BSU. At first, I assumed that students would have great difficulty locating religiously diverse groups in and around Muncie, Indiana. I was wrong.

Students have written ethnographies about: (1) Christianity: Quakers, two Roman Catholic churches, Baptists, a megachurch, Pentecostals, Latter-Day

Saints, Unitarian Universalists, the oldest A.M.E. congregation in Muncie, and a small, socially engaged, urban congregation; (2) a local Islamic Center; (3) Buddhism: Tibetan, Zen, and Burmese/Myanmar Theravada; (4) Bah'ai; (5) Martial Arts as religion; (6) a Spiritualist Church; and (7) Camp Chesterfield, a nationally known Spiritualist Center located near Anderson, Indiana (about a twenty-minute drive from Ball State University). As it turns out, then, one way to connect a "unique contribution" with doing ethnography as a student at Ball State University is linked to the unique opportunities for field research. One could also consider Undergraduate Research generally, or a "unique contribution" specifically in religious studies, as the application of ethnographic methods to write a detailed, self-reflexive ethnographic study of a local religious community. This process teaches the student research methods, theories, and more about "lived religion," all of which are central to the course as I teach it. Although many students were reluctant to engage in field research at first, all of them claimed by the end of the course to have learned far more about their topics than they could have through library research alone. Put differently, students had become empowered through ethnographic study to see religion, themselves, and their perspectives on each transformed over the course of just one semester.

Ethnography as Undergraduate Research: Phase I

In what follows, I insert passages from Nevada's AAR paper to illustrate the process of how she moved from a single course to what I would consider Undergraduate Research. The specific focus of this final paper was the role of play in transmitting religious and cultural knowledge, yet she also writes about the process of becoming an ethnographer. The community she studied is a Burmese (their preferred term, regardless of Burma now "officially" called Myanmar) Theravada community in Fort Wayne, Indiana, a bit over an hour's drive north of Muncie. During her first semester, she traveled and studied there with a partner and was joined by a couple of friends occasionally. This first passage begins with musings about self-reflexivity, which is a learning outcome of the course:

> There is something to be said for the immersive, experiential
> component of learning ethnography, especially as an undergraduate.
> Within the structure of the classroom, it is difficult to have an eye
> toward self-reflexivity. Not so with ethnography. It brings the full
> brunt of experience to bear on expectations. It is rare that students
> are confronted with the weight of their assumptions. The university

is often presented as a virtuous paragon of factual information, students glut themselves on "objective" information, historical, biological, mathematical; these types of knowledge are perceived as unchanging. In the religious studies classroom, using the "world-religions" approach, there is nothing at stake for the student, no catalyst toward deeper understanding of religioning.

As a nascent ethnographer and scholar of religion, I find that documenting this experience self-reflexively and narratively has forced me to dig deeper into the data, to seek, in retrospect, where and how the classroom and field shaped the researcher and, in turn, how I shaped the research. An expectation of objectivity and distance does not help the student of ethnography become more aware of her biases. I hope to explore issues surrounding the experience of learning ethnography, especially with regards to fumbling around during fieldwork, including narratives of those experiences included in my "regular" ethnographic work.

Her reflections, admittedly, were at the end of her sustained engagement with an ethnographic model of research. So, let's back up to the first semester for a moment.[3]

My initial goal was to have students become novice ethnographers. The readings I assigned, however, were heavily theoretical and seem in hindsight to have inhibited the practical, hands-on experience that leads one on the path to becoming an ethnographer. Along the way, I began omitting some readings, incorporating more in-class discussion of their ongoing research, and providing more focused topics for their weekly journals. Initially, the journals were more like response papers to the readings. As I asked specific questions, the journals became the blocks for building students' overall research projects. For example, I might ask: in light of the reading for this week, how has your approach to participant observation and the taking of field notes changed? These are fundamental to ethnographic study, but were useful for students who had "data" but were unsure what to do with it. As we progressed, the questions became more specifically tied to readings in which ethnographers of religion reflected on difficulties and dilemmas they faced while doing research.[4] The possibilities for writing assignments tied to an integrated course design are endless. However, the essays of James V. Spickard, et al. in *Personal Knowledge and Beyond: Reshaping the Ethnography of Religion* and of H. L. Goodall, Jr. in *Writing the New Ethnography* are especially helpful in getting students to reflect on their role as ethnographers in training, especially the impact of their social location on how they frame their research questions and the assumptions that are revealed through this process.[5]

Ethnography as Undergraduate Research: Phase II
(or, a Revised Approach)

My new approach to teaching ethnography the subsequent semester was to have students read several book-length ethnographies. The theoretical issues were still addressed but this time seemed more clearly connected to field research. For their final writing assignments, each student was required to engage with critical issues raised by each of the ethnographies we read. This served two purposes for me: first, it delimited the range of research such that students felt more able to interact with theoretical issues; and second, it showed students that particular ethnographies—or good religious studies texts—always address broader issues than ones directly linked to content. For example, Dawne Moon's *God, Sex and Politics: Homosexuality and Everyday Theologies* (2004) taught students theoretically sophisticated ways of doing ethnographic research in general.[6] Sure, they learned about two Methodist congregations' attempts to grapple with an often-divisive set of issues (i.e., the "content"), but even the content radically challenged taken-for-granted assumptions one might have before reading her text. Nevada noted the following:

> Throughout all the ethnographic research I have read over the course
> of this project, the researchers had some idea of where their views fit.
> In *God, Sex and Politics*, for example, Dawne Moon situates herself
> neatly into the research. She makes her potential biases clearly
> visible.... However, I realize that there are many parts of my own
> background that shape me, and shape how I interact with people.
> I am white. I am female. Further, I am a feminist. I grew up in the
> United States. English is my native language. I have never seen the
> horrors of an oppressive government first hand. I am not religious,
> nor was I raised in any particular religious tradition. I am, at least in
> part, defined by these things. My patterns of thinking are shaped by
> these views, and my responses to field experiences give evidence to
> these things.

These reflections began with responses to ethnography common to many students, namely, fear, lack of direction, uncertainty, and confusion, to name a few. By the end of the course, however, most students had overcome many fears, had gained clarity on a number of issues, yet left the course with just enough confusion to warrant further investigation. These course outcomes are precisely why Undergraduate Research works best when expanded over two or more semesters. While the remaining summaries and excerpts of this one student's work provide my examples of ethnography as Undergraduate Research, most first-time ethnographers experience similar obstacles, insights, and—one hopes—a sense of one's own voice, or empowerment, to move beyond the classroom in the study of religion.

Ethnography as Undergraduate Research: Phase III
(Further Reflections on the Process)

In this section I summarize some of Nevada's reflections as an example of the initial fears and confusion of all ethnographers, as well as include excerpts and comments about her later reflections on becoming an ethnographer. In brief, she wondered about possible communication problems (e.g., would they speak English?), was unsure exactly what it was she wanted to study about the community, and felt like a "foreigner" for the first time in Indiana. She had assumed that discussing the political situation in Burma/Myanmar would be of interest and was shocked to hear there was "no need to do anything" about that. Quickly, she learned, her own interests were shaped by her background and would need to be adjusted if she were to continue with the project. What was key here was that it was her field experience that shaped, and continued to change, her perceptions of herself and the direction of her project. The disjuncture between classroom and the field is indeed central to ethnography:

> The experience of the classroom was vastly different from that of the
> field, and in some ways an inadequate mode of preparation. I do not
> feel that this is by any means the fault of the professor or the class
> structure. Rather, there is some disconnect between the act of
> performing fieldwork and reading about how fieldwork should be
> performed.... No matter how much I tried to stifle it, paranoia floated
> to the surface. Moreover, I had no idea what I wanted to research.
> I feared that my project would turn into a semester spent confused
> and aimless, a terrifying prospect.

This experience often exacerbates one's initial confusion or fear of field research:

> In my case, this took the form of befuddlement regarding interac-
> tions with informants.... Ethnographers were, and to some extent
> still are, expected to maintain some separation. I am pleased that
> there has been a shift in ethnography that is more open to reciprocal

> relationships in the field. I was, and continue to be pleased with
> forming lasting bonds with the children, and even some of the
> adults. I could not resist perceiving these relationships as friendships
> that broke out of the boundaries of a fieldwork relationship. I could
> not pretend not to care about them.

It took quite some time for her to develop the relationships that often occur during fieldwork. Here, the teaching of ethnography has the added benefit of community interaction. By this, I mean that Nevada became more interested in questions that seemed tangential to her research. For example, the more she identified with the "other," the more she felt the need to be an advocate on their behalf against the bigotry she learned of while working with them. Becoming an "advocate" of any sort is not the intention of my teaching ethnography or religious studies; however, such a response fits with increasing attention on many campuses to issues of civic engagement or community relationships.

As with most ethnographic projects, a student's initial research questions and presumed answers are immediately challenged once the fieldwork begins. Usually, this happens with the first site visit, especially when one is able to conduct initial interviews. Nevada began with the question of how Burmese religious and cultural practices were transmitted to younger generations, a topic relevant to any study of a group of recent immigrants. She suspected that teaching Burmese language would be near the top of that list. What she learned from the monks was that the teaching of the Buddha was primary. And they noted that these teachings formed the foundation of morality, or how one ought to behave in culture. Hence, they downplayed the notion of transmitting "Burmese culture," in spite of their own take on Buddhist notions that surely were connected to particular Burmese Theravada traditions. These ideas ultimately resulted in a radically new focus for Nevada's final paper, but there were many other field-related obstacles to negotiate before that point. For example, how to conduct oneself as an English-speaking female interacting with Burmese-speaking persons, especially monks, illustrated the ongoing attention one must have toward learning new (usually unspoken) ways of conducting oneself in public.

These longer excerpts from her paper show the rewards one gains by moving out of the classroom and into the field:

> As an outsider, one of my biggest challenges was not knowing the
> language. As I mentioned before, most conversations at the
> monastery take place in Burmese, unless the community member is
> face-to-face with someone who has no demonstrable skill with the

language. In other words, someone like me. Another challenge I faced was blending in to a community where I am not of the same racial background.... Although no one treated me any differently because of this, it taught me a little bit of what it would be like to be Burmese in Fort Wayne.... However, because of these differences, services at the monastery were shifted for me. *Dhamma* talks (similar to a "sermon") usually given in Burmese were given in English instead. People were assigned to translate for me. My presence interrupted the usual course of the cultural school because the children were showing off for me. Although I tried to make my presence as unobtrusive as possible, there is no doubt that I had affected the study.

There is also no doubt that this study has profoundly affected me. Initially, I feared becoming an advocate. Especially knowing that this project is short-term, I did not want to place myself in the position of desiring to help and support them and not being able to. Further, despite feeling that total objectivity is impossible, I hoped that I could get into the community without getting close to too many of its members. I feel as though I could not have done "my job" properly if I did not get close to these community members and listen to their stories, both of the discrimination they face in America and, sometimes, their desire to return home. I find myself angry when I hear about happenings in Burma, and when I read bigoted letters to the editor [in] local newspapers.

Ethnography, Undergraduate Research, and a Unique Contribution

As mentioned above, one could consider certain semester-long ethnographic research papers to be unique contributions to the field of religious studies. My intention is, however, to set Nevada's work apart from those projects as more appropriately deserving the modifier Undergraduate Research. Her first semester provided ethnographic tools and sufficient fieldwork experience to move that research to a new level of sophistication. When she then continued her research the following semester, her questions were much more focused and were building upon prior experience with the community. The additional readings supplied new theoretical questions that could be applied to previous and ongoing research. Nevada focused her research on children, which allowed her to maintain her initial interest in the transmission of cultural knowledge, yet from a new angle. For the final phase of research—the Independent Study—much of her reading was on two topics: religion and play, as well as autoethnography. This combination narrowed her topic, while also broadening her awareness of the critical issues pertaining to "play" and writing self-reflexively within anthropology. The result of this phase of research was a presentation at the regional AAR meeting in spring 2009.

This entire research process, from my perspective, accomplished far more than was possible in a single-semester course. Nevada learned more about the professional features (e.g., the conference) of our work as scholars of religion and received better training for what lies ahead in graduate school. She gave a version of her AAR paper, accompanied by wonderful pictures and video, at our department's Student Recognition Day in 2009. The process of selecting papers goes through a double-blind review process. Additionally, our faculty unanimously selected Nevada as our Outstanding Senior in Religious Studies for the academic year 2008–09.

My intention throughout Nevada's research was to focus less on the "product" than on the process of doing ethnographic research. That is, I valued the learning, professionalization, and mentoring over the final paper. I do not want, however, to downplay the significance of her final paper as a unique contribution to the field of religious studies. Her work could well be the first ethnographic study of this Burmese Buddhist community in Fort Wayne. Nevada has laid the foundation for further study, whether of the same community, a new one, or even an entirely new direction for graduate school. The institutional location and pedagogical emphases of Ball State University, again, provided her the opportunity for Undergraduate Research using an ethnographic model. The adaptability of this model surely fits other institutions' goals for implementing Undergraduate Research in religious studies.

Student Reflections on Ethnography

Nevada Drollinger

To be sure, this experience has colored both my quotidian and academic worlds. I cannot say how different my experience might have been had I been able to situate myself into my research self-reflexively and were I not introduced to anthropologists, sociologists and scholars of religion who do the same. Ultimately, I have found this emphasis on placing myself and my history into the scope of my work a most rewarding experience, both for learning the practice of ethnography and the complexity of the study of religion.

NOTES

1. Karen O'Reilly, *Ethnographic Methods* (London: Routledge, 2005), 3.

2. I would like to thank Chava Weissler (Lehigh University) and Clark Chilson (University of Pittsburgh) for sharing their ideas and syllabi with me for their "Ethnography of Religion" seminars. Both have had an influence on how I continue to envision, revise, and teach this course.

3. For course design, I drew heavily from L. Dee Fink's *Creating Significant Learning Experiences: An Integrated Approach to Designing College Courses* (San Francisco: Jossey-Bass, 2003), 63ff., especially his notion of "backward design." The basic idea here is to ask what it is you (the instructor) want a student to be at the end of your course. More difficult still, what do you want students to remember from your course several years later? Fink's approach is clearly learning centered, not content centered.

4. H. L. Goodall, Jr. helps students become ethnographers by working on the following:

> You have to learn how to do fieldwork.
> You have to learn how to write.
> You have to learn who you are as a fieldworker, as a writer, and as a self.
> And you have to learn how—and where—those activities are meaningfully connected.

H. L. Goodall, Jr., *Writing the New Ethnography* (Walnut Creek, CA: AltaMira Press, 2000), 7.

5. James V. Spickard, J. Shawn Landres, and Meredith B. McGuire, eds., *Personal Knowledge and Beyond: Reshaping the Ethnography of Religion* (New York: NYU Press, 2002); Goodall, "Writing the New Ethnography".

6. Dawne Moon, *God, Sex and Politics: Homosexuality and Everyday Theologies* (Chicago: University of Chicago Press, 2004).

8

Examining History

David C. Ratke

I am a professor of religion at Lenoir-Rhyne University, a church-related institution. My training and scholarly interests are primarily in theology—in contemporary systematic theology to be precise. The religion curriculum at Lenoir-Rhyne does not focus on my interests so much as on the history of theology or the history of Christianity. Consequently the interests of many of my students who choose to undertake Undergraduate Research are shaped and informed by their course work in history of Christian thought. Happily I like history. I never did any significant Undergraduate Research myself. At least I didn't do Undergraduate Research as the contributors to this volume understand it. Central to our notion of Undergraduate Research is mentoring. Certainly, I wrote essays and papers at the University of Alberta during my undergraduate studies, but those essays were always for and within courses. In fact, I can count on one hand the number of times that I spoke to a professor about an essay I was working on either after class or during office hours. My understanding of Undergraduate Research is shaped by my experience of my graduate school experiences. That is something that I always need to keep in mind. While there are some similarities between the two, Undergraduate Research is not graduate research!

What Is a "Historical" Project?

While I teach history and mentor students in historical research in the field of religious studies, I don't think of myself as a historian in any sense. I'm a systematic theologian interested primarily in contemporary theology, and my work largely reflects that. That said, I am interested in history. I am interested in the historical context of religious figures and movements.

To understand the Reformation, for example, I think that it's helpful, perhaps even necessary, for students to understand the impact that Guttenberg's printing press had; the impact that driving the Arabs out of Spain had; the differences between Wittenberg, Zurich, and Geneva and how their political, cultural, and social contexts had particular influences on Luther, Zwingli, and Calvin. Does it make a difference that Ignatius of Loyola was a Spanish soldier? I think so. Loyola was a committed Roman Catholic. Would he have been so committed to Roman Catholicism had Spain not been recently reclaimed by a Spanish Catholic monarchy?

The work of Mary Daly and Rosemary Radford Ruether and Elisabeth Schüssler Fiorenza cannot be understood apart from the women's movement for equal rights that emerged in the 1960s. The work of Gustavo Gutiérrez and Leonardo Boff and Ernesto Cardenal cannot be understood apart from the national independence movements that arose following World War II. The work of James Cone and Albert J. Raboteau and Albert Cleage cannot be understood apart from the civil rights movement of the 1960s.

A historical approach to religious studies seeks to understand the historical context of a religious figure or movement. Leopold von Ranke's principle that history should describe it "wie es eigentlich gewesen" (how it really or actually was) is probably unattainable. Nonetheless history that seeks only to show what actually happened is an ideal to strive for even as we know that there are limitations.

That we cannot know what actually happened in a complete way should not prevent us from trying. For that reason a historical approach is characterized by the endeavor to understand the influences that shape a figure or movement. Students (or an experienced scholar) might limit themselves to a particular influence or constellation of influences upon a figure. One thinks, for example, of Erik Erikson's *Young Man Luther*, which seeks to understand Luther from the perspective of psychology. This kind of limit on a project is a perfectly legitimate limitation presuming, of course, that one doesn't presume that it provides *the* perspective. Such a presumption is contrary to the academic enterprise that is always aware of its own limitations and uncertainties.

Limiting ourselves to one perspective on a figure or movement certainly narrows our understanding in one sense, but in another sense it allows us to examine all the nooks and crannies within the perspective. Such a detailed examination can illuminate connections and knowledge hitherto unknown.

Independent Undergraduate Research: Vincent

One of the operating assumptions of the Working Group on Undergraduate Research in Religious Studies is that Undergraduate Research can be initiated either by me (the professor) or by the student. For example, in a recent course I taught, Medieval Christian Thought, we read *Cur Deus Homo* by Anselm of Canterbury. Vincent was one of the students in that class.[1] He came to Lenoir-Rhyne from Florida and was attracted to the institution because of its religious affiliation as well as the opportunity to play baseball. I suspect that four years ago baseball mattered more. In any case, he started out as a math major and for a variety of reasons (not the least of which was the difficulty of fitting classes into his baseball schedule) changed his major to religion. Did I mention he is also in the honors program? Vincent is gregarious and curious. One day after class, he mentioned to me that he planned to write his term paper on Anselm and asked for some advice on where to start. We talked a little and I gave him some suggestions for secondary literature to look at. He wrote the paper and did a pretty good job of it. There was a tendency to wordiness that I would have liked him to tidy up, but that's part of the learning process. In general, the paper was researched thoroughly and written thoughtfully. That is to say, it was a very good, even excellent, but not outstanding paper. Vincent is a student that I could work with. He's interested, motivated, and industrious.

Sometime during the next semester, he came to me and asked about further research in the topic of atonement. We talked more and we agreed that he would do some further reading in the summer on the topic. I pointed him to a couple of resources, one of which was Gustaf Aulén's *Christus Victor*. At the beginning of the next fall semester, Vincent dropped by once again and informed me that he had devoured the readings on atonement and was even more interested in the topic. As he told me, "When I wrote the paper on Anselm, I thought that I understood it well enough to claim it as my own. I want to do that with Irenaeus."

Some Barriers

At this declaration I was faced with a decision, a crisis. I've read Irenaeus, but it has been a really long time. More than that, I had not read much of him. What to do? In the end, I said to Vincent, "I'm willing to supervise your reading of Irenaeus. I can be a sounding board as you attempt to work out what he's saying and you try to understand it. However I have neither the background nor the time and energy right now to walk you through it." Even with these limitations Vincent said yes.

There are other limitations that I didn't mention but thought of. Most of us who have done doctoral work, particularly in historical theology, believe that you ought to read the sources in the original language. Irenaeus wrote in Latin. Vincent is a pretty smart and motivated student, but it seemed unreasonable to ask him to learn Latin so that he can follow his passion for Irenaeus. My own opinion is to let his passion for Irenaeus move him to learn Latin so that he can read Irenaeus in his own tongue and thereby appreciate Irenaeus all the more.

Probably the first barrier that Vincent and I encountered was me. As a scholar in the humanities I was not trained to work collaboratively in teams. I can recall my friends at the University of Alberta who majored in engineering and regularly did group projects. They were socialized into patterns of work that they would later encounter in their careers. As a student I never worked with other students. As a scholar I have never coauthored anything with anybody.

The next challenge was that of literature. I could point him to some general reference works and introductions. He read the entry on Irenaeus in *The First Christian Theologians* edited by G. R. Evans. I told him to track down the entries in the bibliography in that article. He did that. But it's at this point that Vincent and I were confronted with two challenges. First, our library is not a research library; it is a teaching library. Very few of the books and articles mentioned in the encyclopedia entries and historical introductions are available in our library. These specialized resources are actually readily available on interlibrary loan, but that process seems rather archaic and weird to someone raised on the immediacy of the Internet. Vincent however, as I mentioned, is nothing if not teachable. So I walked him through the interlibrary loan process.

Another challenge is finding resources. Vincent is accustomed to using Google to find resources. He knows about electronic archives such as those from ProQuest Research Library, Academic Search Premier from EBSCOhost, and JSTOR. He is not particularly accustomed or comfortable with using them, but he knows about them. Because he has not used them much, he does not know how to use them to their full potential and power. This is part of the learning process that is central to Undergraduate Research: learning how to use new tools to their fullest power. In my classes, I give students an assignment, the library resource hunt, that is intended to begin to address this challenge in the context of the classroom. The undergraduate engaging in research will need further guidance from a faculty mentor in finding resources.

I suspect that for many of us who have earned research doctorates, we have fond memories of many hours browsing in the library stacks, finding some gem, and making connections between ideas and figures and movements. I recall digging around in the stacks in the library at the Graduate Theological Union in Berkeley and discovering that Paul Tillich and H. Richard Niebuhr reviewed each other's books. Or that they knew and read some of the same people. Who could not tell a story of discovering somebody they did not know about or an idea they were not aware of because a book happened to be in the next bookcase over or the bookcase behind where you were standing. Most academics view libraries as temples waiting to reveal wondrous mysteries. That is what I want Vincent to discover. That's hard, however. Students of Vincent's generation are not as accustomed to browsing through the stacks just to see what comes up. And yet, I think that is an essential part of doing historical or archival research. Much of it is dusty, tedious, laborious work. Much of it, quite frankly, is not fun. And yet, it is so satisfying when the lightbulb goes on simply because it is laborious, tedious, and dusty.

These are challenges and perhaps even barriers. They are also why Undergraduate Research even at small universities and colleges like Lenoir-Rhyne is so important. Consider this last challenge: introducing students to the pleasures of foraging around in the library stacks. To be a scholar, an academic, is not just a job, it is an identity. It is to understand yourself as somebody who still has something to learn and to discover and to encounter. One of my goals in working with a student like Vincent is to impart to him an identity he can grow into even if he does not become a professional academic as I am. I want him to appreciate the unity and interconnectedness of knowledge. I want him to follow his curiosity and see what discoveries he makes.

I mentioned at the outset that the smallness of our library might be an asset.[2] As an undergraduate, I attended the University of Alberta, a large research university of perhaps 30,000 students. The humanities library alone (there was also an undergraduate library, a science library, a social sciences library, an education library—you get the idea) was four or five times the size of the library at Lenoir-Rhyne. When I was an undergraduate, I was assigned to write an essay once on Karl Marx. I was overwhelmed by the books written on Marx, nevermind the books written by Marx. I thought, "There's no way I can possibly write comprehensively on the man much less research him." That is not as likely to be a problem for our students. Our students are less likely to be overwhelmed by the size of our holdings on a particular figure, topic, or era than by the challenge of getting their hands on useful resources. Moreover our librarians are just as accessible to Vincent as I am.

Benefits to Undergraduate Research in Religious History:
Or Why History?

One reason to encourage a student to undertake Undergraduate Research is so that student can learn and understand the interconnectedness and interplay of historical events. The world is a big place. As specialists we sometimes forget that. Our task as educators and mentors is to introduce students to the wonderful immensity of the world. Consider Paul Tillich for a moment. He was a chaplain in World War I and was terribly scarred and traumatized by that experience. Later in 1933, he was among the very first professors to be removed from their chairs when Hitler and his henchmen seized control of the German government. Tillich understood the horrible and terrible threat that Hitler posed to European intellectual and cultural life. He stood up and opposed Hitler and paid a price for opposition. He was removed from his professorship and exiled. None of this is particularly apparent if you simply read his major writings like *Systematic Theology*, *The Courage to Be*, *The Dynamics of Faith*, and so forth. In fact, it is hardly apparent unless you read his personal correspondence or perhaps his mostly unpublished radio addresses. For all of that, it is difficult to understand the political, social, and cultural force of his work unless you are aware of the historical context. And it hardly stops there. My point is that for Vincent to understand Irenaeus, there is so much more for him to do than simply read Irenaeus deeply and closely. He needs to know something about Irenaeus' contemporaries, about the political and cultural and social and economic situation of Irenaeus' world.

Understanding the historical context has another purpose as well. One of the virtues of the humanities is that it builds and maintains "the cultural memory of the human race."[3] Vincent, by learning about Irenaeus's historical context, helps preserve the memory of Irenaeus and his context. In any case, we began work in autumn in an independent study course. My thought was to model my own research process.[4] We began by reading some material in general reference works and then followed the citations and bibliography to more specialized and focused material.[5] Along the way, we made notes about what we read. The notes, I said, would be of two types: (1) quotes and summaries of material that seemed important; and (2) our own reactions to what we read. I showed Vincent my own notes and required him to write at least two pages of notes each week. In fact, he produced much more. The requirement was easily met. After reading some selections from general reference works but before digging into the more specialized treatments of Irenaeus, we read Irenaeus himself. The specialized treatments of Irenaeus were used to clarify questions we might have or to raise questions that we had not considered.

The most immediately obvious benefit was that Vincent experienced what it is like to be a scholar. To most students the life of a professor is like that of a student: go to class, perhaps read a few pages (or maybe a lot of pages), hang out with friends, and occasionally write a paper. Vincent discovered that the reality is quite different and how to appreciate it.[6] Being a professor and an active scholar is hard work. You spend a lot of time simply chasing down leads, some of which are red herrings. It is difficult and often unrewarding. Vincent also discovered that because it is difficult and often unrewarding, it is all the more satisfying when you discover something new. Vincent also discovered that scholarly work in the humanities is fundamentally a solitary endeavor.[7] I tried to make the project as collaborative and communal as possible. I wanted Vincent to "practice" at being a scholar. I wanted him to experience what it is like to search for useful works, to labor over one paragraph or even one sentence. As David Chapman phrases it, I wanted Vincent to "learn the conventions of research through imitation and practice."[8] Vincent and I shared our frustrations and our accomplishments. We commiserated with each other. We read each other's work and so forth. Nonetheless the essence of our work as scholars is reading, hours and hours of reading. Most scholars I know do not read out loud to each other. They might bounce ideas off each other, push each other, but they do not read texts out loud to each other. That is to say that the bulk of our research is solitary reading. The bulk of our research is spent wandering through the library, perusing volumes that may not further our work, and simply reading. The writing is fundamentally solitary as well. Vincent discovered that being a scholar is working alone. It is working independently.

By "simply reading," I mean that I might suggest some text or another to Vincent. He would read that text and we would meet. I'd ask, "What questions does this text raise for you?" I would also ask, "Did you find anything interesting or informative?" In each of these cases after we discussed his responses and discussed further avenues of research, I'd tell him, "Follow the footnotes." His job was to track the information and use those sources as a way of gathering information or analyses. Our discussion of his writing went in similar directions. He would walk me through his drafts, and I would ask questions about the flow of his argument, about the reliability of his sources, and about where a certain text of Irenaeus fit into his argument.

This was essentially the routine throughout the entire research process. Vincent started with a topic (atonement). From that topic he moved to a question: how have Christian theologians besides Anselm thought about atonement? That question became even narrower: how did Irenaeus think about the work of Christ? Once Vincent settled on this still relatively broad question, he could read more critically. I regularly pressed Vincent to be on the alert for contradictions, inconsistencies, and disagreements he had with Irenaeus and his analysts. One way, I told him, to think about the process of research was to think of it as a conversation: What questions would you ask Irenaeus if you could? How are his analysts and commentators getting him wrong? How do they get Irenaeus right? What issues do they raise? After having read (and written) a fair bit on Irenaeus, what would you say about him in a sentence? This last question was meant to push Vincent to think about what claim he wants to make. Then, after deciding what he might want to say about Irenaeus, what problem does this solve? Identifying this problem will often cause a scholar to go back and examine how others have thought about and responded to this problem.

Mostly, however, I want Vincent to think about what he wants to say about Irenaeus and how he wants to say it. His task is twofold: to find evidence for his argument and to develop a structure that's reasonable for that argument. He needs to finds quotes and statements from Irenaeus and then to present them in a structured way that makes sense. However, he's not just presenting Irenaeus's argument again. He's presenting it in a way that responds to the problem that Vincent has identified. This means moving from problem to claim in a systematic, logical, and structured way. It means providing evidence for each of his argumentative moves as he proceeds from problem to claim.

One of the important tasks in this process is recognizing assumptions and presuppositions. I push Vincent to consider how others might see his work. How might someone from a background and context rather different from his react and respond to Vincent's claims and arguments? How might such a person view the evidence that Vincent presents? Would they organize it in a similar way? These are all questions that are intended to push Vincent to come clean with his own presuppositions.

Vincent discovered that he could be, that he is, a scholar. He came to Lenoir-Rhyne to play baseball. If you asked him when he first arrived what his gifts were, he would have said that he can hit and throw a baseball. Only secondarily would he have replied that he was smart. By working on a longer and deeper project he gained confidence in himself and his academic abilities.

As he said, "When I wrote that paper on Anselm, I felt like I made Anselm my own, that I truly understood him."

Maybe Vincent made Anselm and later Irenaeus "his own." That is another discussion. In fact, I think that if you were to ask Vincent about either Anselm or Irenaeus, he would say that he is much more aware of what he does not know than before. While he knows more about both Anselm and Irenaeus and about Christology and soteriology and doctrines of atonement, he is also aware of the limitations of his knowledge. It is truer to say that he has made the identity of researcher or scholar his own. Before that was an identity that he could have only caught fleeting glimpses of; now that is an identity that he can more confidently claim as one that is rightfully his.

Lessons Learned

I write this entire chapter with some hesitation. My own experience with supervising Undergraduate Research is hit and miss. I've learned some things along the way. Undergraduate Research is demanding. It demands much of the student. I find that intellectual ability is less important for student success than perseverance and persistence. I don't want to discount intellectual ability, because it is important. However in a project that runs at least one semester (the thesis projects that I generally supervise are two semesters), persistence and perseverance are necessary. Students have to be able to keep plugging away. It is, I tell students, like that old saying: How do you eat an elephant? One bite at a time. You write a thesis one sentence at a time. And you research that thesis one article or chapter at a time.

Undergraduate Research is demanding in another way as well. Vincent asked me to help him with Irenaeus and atonement. You might remember that I said yes even though I didn't feel entirely competent in Irenaeus. I told Vincent that I could really only act as a sounding board. In fact, I ended up doing much more. More recently I've been more restrictive with students. They must do research in a field that I either am quite familiar with or am engaged in research of my own. I define "fields that I'm quite familiar with" as thinkers or topics I've written on (e.g., my master's thesis and doctoral dissertation). Sometimes it might be someone or something I'm familiar with through my own teaching (although this is less common).

At any given time, I generally have two or three research projects of my own. If a student is interested in one of those, it works nicely for me because it gives me a push to keep at it (that's the persistence and perseverance thing I mentioned earlier). Undergraduate Research is extra to what I normally do.

I teach at an institution where faculty teach four courses each semester. I'm trying to keep up a modest research program as well as teach conscientiously. All of these contractual responsibilities are balanced against my familial and community responsibilities as well. In short, working with an individual student is demanding enough that I need for that Undergraduate Research supervision to fit in with what I'm already doing or have done. I don't have a lot of extra time and energy for Undergraduate Research.

Even with these limitations, I find that students still welcome the opportunity to work alongside me. Knowing that they're shaping and contributing to my thinking about my own work is an incentive.

Being explicit about my own limitations and restrictions with students is helpful in another way as well. I find that I'm increasingly insistent at the front end of a project about maintaining deadlines. I insist that students meet with me regularly (usually weekly and never less than biweekly). When they meet with me, I insist on progress reports and updates. If they can't maintain this pace, I'll abort the project before they get so far behind that they can't possibly complete it. I'll negotiate a withdrawal from the independent study course at the first—well, maybe the second—sign of trouble.

I suppose the bottom line is this: be clear about your own limitations and be prepared to enforce those. Also be clear about your student's aptitude for Undergraduate Research.

Conclusion

In the end, Vincent didn't complete the project that he began. He realized that it was bigger than he thought and that he would be hard-pressed to see it through to completion. That's not a bad thing. He learned his own limitations even while learning something about his own abilities. He learned that his abilities were far beyond what he imagined. Vincent knew and understood my (and the academy's) expectations. He discovered that he could probably meet them. He also discovered that at that moment in his life—because of *his* historical context—he needed to let the project go.

This discovery of himself and his own abilities is something that I hope that every student who engages in Undergraduate Research will experience. This is a clear and tangible benefit for students. Also clear and tangible is the interconnectedness of our lives and that of the religious figures and movements we study. Our ideas and knowledge are shaped by forces known and unknown, visible and invisible, to us and the subjects of our inquiry. Our lives and our knowledge, students learn, are partial and incomplete.

Whatever students produce reaches to something that is beyond their own estimation of their abilities. Whatever they produce invariably begins to look like something that an experienced scholar would recognize as kin to his or her own work. The student's product may not be quite as comprehensive or polished, but it looks like it belongs. This is the value and benefit of Undergraduate Research: students realize the possibility that they and their scholarship do belong in the academy.

Student Reflection on Developing Research and Writing Skills

Elizabeth Dunnam

Once I decided on the topic that I wanted to research and began this process, the natural desire to say something original and of significance followed. It is important with a research paper to avoid simply reporting the material researched. A research paper is not a book report. A research paper gives the student an opportunity to speak his or her own thoughts. The student must ask, "What do I think about this material, and how does it support or contradict what I want to say?" This leads to the development of a strong thesis which structures and conducts the body of the paper. A research paper is not about brains or wit, but more importantly, it is about passion and a desire to speak one's mind.

NOTES

1. "Vincent" is based on an actual student; however I have borrowed freely from my experience with other students.

2. Neal B. Abraham, "Facilities and Resources That Promote a Research-Supportive Curriculum," in *Developing and Sustaining a Research-Supportive Curriculum: A Compendium of Successful Practices*, ed. Kerry K. Karukstis and Timothy E. Elgren (Washington, DC: Council on Undergraduate Research, 2007), 485 observes that "a study of the facilities at colleges and universities where faculty members and students are research active reveals that energy, imagination, and commitment can offset many facility deficiencies."

3. David N. DeVries, "Undergraduate Research in the Humanities: An Oxymoron?" *CUR Quarterly* 21, no. 4 (June 2001): 154.

4. V. Daniel Rogers describes a similar approach; see V. Daniel Rogers, "Surviving the 'Culture Shock' of Undergraduate Research in the Humanities," *CUR Quarterly* 23, no. 3 (March 2003): 134. Also, Joyce Kinkead reports that undergraduate research benefi ts students defined as at risk or underrepresented in the field; see

Joyce Kinkead, "Learning Through Inquiry: An Overview of Undergraduate Research," in *Valuing and Supporting Undergraduate Research*, ed. Joyce Kinkead, special issue, *New Directions for Teaching and Learning* 93 (Spring 2003): 11.

5. This is an approach also recommended in Wayne C. Booth, Gregory G. Colomb, and Joseph M. Williams, *The Craft of Research*, 2nd ed. (Chicago: University of Chicago Press, 2003), 79–89, esp. 88; see also Kate L. Turabian, *A Manual For Writers of Research Papers, Theses, and Dissertations*, 7th ed., rev. Wayne C. Booth and Gregory G. Colomb, Joseph M. Williams (Chicago: University of Chicago Press, 2007), 32.

6. David Lopatto in his study reaches similar conclusions; see David Lopatto, "The Essential Features of Undergraduate Research," *CUR Quarterly* 23, no. 3 (March 2003): 140; also John Ishiyama, "Does Early Participation in Undergraduate Research Benefit Social Science and Humanities Students?" *College Student Journal* 36, no. 3 (September 2002): 381–7.

7. Todd McDorman. "Promoting Undergraduate Research in the Humanities: Three Collaborative Approaches," *CUR Quarterly* 25, no. 1 (September 2004): 39 makes a similar observation.

8. David W. Chapman, "Undergraduate Research: Showcasing Young Scholars" in *The Chronicle of Higher Education* 50, no. 3 (12 September 2003): B5.

9

Working with Texts

Lynn R. Huber and Robin Rinehart

At first glance, religious studies scholars whose work focuses upon original texts might balk at the idea of mentoring Undergraduate Research. We have been trained to work with texts in their original and often ancient languages and to acknowledge the traces of complex reception histories in our own readings. Some of us have built our careers around arguing for or against preferred readings based upon supposedly misplaced vowel points or newly discovered papyri. Whether the texts to which we devote our scholarly attentions are in Arabic or Greek, Hebrew or Sanskrit, Coptic or Latin, it can be daunting for us to imagine "translating" our work into a format that undergraduates can manage on their own. This difficulty is only heightened for some when we assume the definition of Undergraduate Research as making an original contribution to the field of religious studies, the working assumption for this volume. As the popularity of Undergraduate Research spreads among colleges and universities, more of us will be encouraged by administrators, students, and faculty colleagues to follow the leads of the natural and social sciences in offering our students Undergraduate Research opportunities. In fact, many of our institutions promote Undergraduate Research to faculty by highlighting the ways it intersects with the research that faculty already are doing or want to spend more time doing. The growing assumption that we should be offering our students research opportunities underscores the question of how to do Undergraduate Research in fields that traditionally presume knowledge of an ancient or not commonly taught language.

In light of this, we will explore some of the ways those of us in textually based fields might pursue Undergraduate Research. We will do so by drawing upon our experiences of Undergraduate Research, which reflect our distinct fields. Robin's work focuses on the religious literature of the Punjab region of the Indian subcontinent, and Lynn's research is primarily in the field of New Testament. In both cases, we teach at institutions—Lafayette College and Elon University respectively—that emphasize Undergraduate Research as distinctive features of their academic offerings. Similarly, and like Undergraduate Research programs in general, our institutions have developed their Undergraduate Research programs from a model emerging out of the natural and social sciences. While Lynn has found it possible to work within the Undergraduate Research program at Elon, it has in some ways been more difficult for Robin to integrate into her institutional program. However, we are both committed to exploring ways of mentoring undergraduates, formally or informally, in our respective fields. By sharing our experiences, positive and negative, we will highlight some strategies for, and difficulties with, doing Undergraduate Research in textually based fields.

Case Study #1: Robin

Our religious studies major at Lafayette College requires that students either complete a one-semester "capstone" research project or a two-semester honors thesis project in their senior year. We tell our students that the capstone or thesis requirement gives them the chance to design a project in an area of their own interest and that we expect that the final product will demonstrate the results of the student's research and include some attention to matters of theory and method. Most capstone students choose to work with a faculty member whose own expertise is in the area in which they plan to do their project. Most students produce a written paper and present their work to departmental faculty and other students at the end of the semester. Students completing honors have a formal thesis committee with an advisor, second departmental member, and an outside member, and they defend their thesis at the end of their senior year. In addition to presenting their work to Lafayette faculty and students, some of our majors have given presentations based on their research at a local Undergraduate Women's Studies Conference and at the National Conferences on Undergraduate Research (NCUR). At Lafayette, many departments, especially in the natural sciences and engineering, encourage and even require junior faculty to involve students in their own research. Faculty publications with student coauthors are highly valued for tenure and promotion. The EXCEL

Scholars Program at Lafayette provides funding for students who work on research with faculty members. Typical of many Undergraduate Research programs, it is conceptualized in language most appropriate for scientific research: "You are challenged to make a significant contribution and are involved in all aspects of the research from reading and analyzing articles to designing experiments, testing hypotheses, interpreting data, and writing articles about the results for publication."[1] Colleagues in the humanities have been reluctant to nominate students to work with them as EXCEL Scholars because they believe that undergraduates have neither the linguistic skills nor disciplinary sophistication to make significant contributions to faculty research. Because the number of humanities faculty participating in the program has been relatively low, Lafayette is considering changing the program so that students working with humanities faculty may be designated as "research assistants" rather than potential coauthors. Although every year several students contact me asking me whether they might work with me as EXCEL Scholars, I have not yet found a student with sufficient knowledge either of Indian languages or the field of religious studies to make a project feasible. As a result, I have focused on mentoring capstone and honors thesis projects in my own department, but not projects that are part of my own research program.

The example I will discuss here is from a capstone project, and the student, Todd (who kindly agreed to let me share this account of his project), presented his work at the National Conferences on Undergraduate Research (NCUR) in 2009. I first met with Todd in the spring of his junior year. He knew he had to fulfill the capstone requirement and wanted to get started on his research over the summer. He had taken two courses in Indian religion as well as our Theories of Religion course and was broadly interested in the idea of how humans establish a connection with the divine. He wanted to explore this theme through art or literature related to the Hindu god Krishna. We worked together to develop a preliminary summer reading list that included works on the mythology of Krishna and classical Indian aesthetic theory. No Indian language instruction is offered at Lafayette, and Todd had no knowledge of any of the Indian languages in which the texts relevant to his area of interest are composed. The project he envisioned spanned texts in both Sanskrit and Indian vernacular languages. Fortunately many excellent English translations and scholarly studies of literature related to Krishna are available. This meant that Todd was able to pursue a textual studies project based solely on literature in translation. Had he chosen an area in which there were not so many translations available, the project might not have been feasible.

Early in the fall, Todd met with me to talk about what he had learned over the summer. He realized that he wanted to narrow his focus to literature rather than art and was most interested in vernacular devotional poetry. Over the course of the semester, Todd and I met every week or so to talk about his progress. Initially, I asked him to prepare written summaries of the material he was reading each week and also to write a paragraph outlining the ideas that most interested him. He revised and expanded this paragraph over several weeks, and it became the basis for his project outline and helped him decide what materials to focus on and in what order.

Todd's interest in vernacular devotional poetry gave us the opportunity to talk about many issues central to the study of Indian religious texts. He ended up focusing on poetry to Krishna (in translation) composed in Bengali and Brajbhasha, two north Indian languages. These poems, however, build upon mythology from classical Sanskrit texts. Thus Todd thought about the nature of the relationship between classical texts and more accessible vernacular texts. These poems are also connected to different sectarian theological traditions in Hinduism; Todd as a result read about two different sectarian theologies focused on Krishna and how those theologies are expressed in poetry. The recitation and performance of the poems take place in a context influenced both by ritual practices and aesthetic theory (particularly the concept of *rasa* or "mood," according to which a poem, musical piece, or other artistic performance evokes a specific mood). We thus identified both primary and secondary texts in each of these areas and developed a reading and writing schedule so that Todd's final paper could address each of these issues in turn. While there was ample material translated into English available for each of these issues, as the project developed, Todd began to see some of the limitations of working with texts in translation, particularly in the case of the poems themselves, because the translators made clear what was lost in translation. He also recognized the importance of consulting original texts and not just summaries of such texts in secondary literature; I was especially impressed toward the end of the semester when he asked to borrow a translation of a Bengali poet's biography because he wanted to make sure it had been accurately represented in the secondary materials that had referred to it. Todd's focus on devotional poetry in two different languages also highlighted for him the regional variations within Hindu tradition.

Late that fall, I encouraged Todd to submit a proposal to the National Conferences on Undergraduate Research to present his work that spring; his proposal was successful, and Lafayette College provided funding for him to attend the conference. Todd also presented a summary of his work to religious studies faculty and majors at the end of the semester. It was without doubt a successful project. As Todd made the final revisions to his paper, he told me that he had learned more about research and writing with this project than anything else he had done so far in college. That was of course gratifying to me as his mentor and made me reflect on what about the project was so valuable for Todd. First, I think there was a real sense of accomplishment at having written something much longer and more substantive than typical research papers for classes. Second, he had had the freedom to pursue his own interests as he shaped the project, and while we frequently spoke about how he might proceed, it was up to Todd to make the choices about which sources to focus on and how to connect the different parts of the paper.

For some, the fact that Todd's work was based entirely on English-language materials might mitigate against the claim that this project made an original or creative contribution to the field. I myself have struggled with this oft-cited criterion for Undergraduate Research, and in one of our Working Group's early discussions I argued that perhaps it is best to view Undergraduate Research in religious studies as making an original or creative contribution to the field relative to the work of other undergraduates doing research in religious studies (see chapter 2 for a more detailed discussion of this proposal). In studies of texts in languages other than English, there will always be limitations to projects that rely on those texts in translation rather than in their original language. But this of course should not mean that we discourage such projects. Textual studies Undergraduate Research projects in religious studies can serve as a bridge between undergraduate- and graduate-level work. If a student such as Todd were to go on to graduate school in religious studies, a project such as the one he completed would have made clear to him the necessity of learning primary languages in order to do original research. I believe that this realization in and of itself is a significant accomplishment and one of the many things that makes Undergraduate Research in religious studies worthwhile.

Case Study #2: Lynn

One of my initial forays into Undergraduate Research was as a mentor for a history student interested in exploring the biblical traditions used to justify the First Crusade. His project was part of the Elon College Fellows program, which requires students to engage in an Undergraduate Research project conducted over at least two semesters. The experience ideally culminates in "a professional product or body of work commensurate with the discipline or academic major" and requires a public presentation of the student's work.[2] Since this student was unable to find a medieval historian to work with on his project, he turned to the religious studies department and was eventually directed to me since I occasionally teach a course in ancient and medieval Christianity and have done some research on medieval interpretations of the Bible. Not having worked with

Undergraduate Research in any significant way and eager to make a good impression as a new faculty person at my institution, I agreed to mentor the project. The student was enthusiastic as he assured me that he had taken Latin in high school. As we began to outline the project together, it became clear that the student's background in Latin was limited. Nor did he have enough familiarity working with texts in translation to ask the questions necessary to get at the text "behind" the translation. While a more experienced faculty person might have anticipated this, it was a surprise for me as a new teacher. To address this, I had to spend valuable time working through texts with the student to assist him as he moved between the Latin to the English translation. More important, the linguistic connections between the ancient and the medieval texts were vague, and his untrained ear was not able to catch any potential similarities between the rhetoric employed in the biblical texts and in the speech of Pope Urban II at the Council of Clermont, for instance. Most of the connections that the student found were those suggested in secondary sources or by me. Likewise, he found it difficult to think about how the appropriation of a text into a new rhetorical context altered its meaning. His tendency was to locate the text's meaning primarily within the original context and to read the original context into the new textual setting. In sum, while this student was a strong student, he simply did not possess the background to engage in original textual or historical work on this topic. I had made a "rookie mistake" in agreeing to mentor the student in this particular project, mistaking eagerness for skill and not realizing that most undergraduates would not have enough background for such a sophisticated textual project. Among other things, this experience points to the importance of taking a fair amount of time to assess a student's abilities, including language abilities, before agreeing to work with him or her on a particular topic.

After this initial attempt at Undergraduate Research, I have encouraged research students to explore interpretations of biblical texts in "languages" with which they are more familiar, whether the language is visual art, popular culture, feminist thought, or another mode of discourse. By exploring how a particular text or a set of related texts is appropriated into another language with which the student is more familiar, the student is able to explore the complexities of textual "translation" or "interpretation" without having had years of Hebrew, Greek, or Latin. This does not preclude the student's becoming familiar with the major exegetical issues; however, these linguistic complexities are not the basis around which the student conducts research. Additionally, by examining how texts have been interpreted through this other mode of discourse, students are able to engage in original research, research that is not dependent upon the insights of others, but involves the student's own analysis, which is one of the expectations of Undergraduate Research.

One example of having a student explore the translation of ancient texts into a more familiar vernacular is a student, Erin, who examined the appropriation of Lilith traditions in popular feminist settings. Specifically, Erin examined how the ancient traditions about Lilith get reworked, emended, and even simplified in contemporary feminist appropriations, such as Lilith Fair and online shrines devoted to the ancient Jewish "demoness." Drawing upon a range of feminist historical scholarship, Erin developed and applied criteria for assessing "responsible" readings of the ancient traditions. This allowed her to analyze and assess modern readings of the tradition. Since Erin's focus was on contemporary readings and not ancient or historical appropriations of the text, some of the pressure of working with ancient texts in Hebrew was mitigated.

Although Erin's project was aimed at understanding contemporary readings, she did devote a significant amount of time and effort examining the ancient textual traditions about Lilith. This required Erin to have a basic knowledge of how translation works, text criticism, and ancient Jewish interpretive practices. Obviously, we spent a good deal of time working through these issues together, as it was necessary to teach her about working with critical translations, academic commentaries, and other tools of the trade. In other words, we had to move beyond just comparing different English translations with the Hebrew text. Among the easier issues for Erin to grasp was the variety of translations a text can yield. Like many other students today, Erin had experience in learning a foreign language, and she was able to draw on that experience to help her. Students who have taken a number of years of Spanish or French or another language can be reminded that just as there are multiple ways of communicating a thought in one of these modern languages, such is the case in ancient languages. The nature of Lilith traditions meant that Erin also had to investigate some of the complex issues around dating texts and traditions, including Rabbinic traditions and the *Alphabet of Ben Sira*. In a world in which copyright dates are routinely published in a book's front matter, students often think that tasks like identifying the date of a text should be relatively straightforward; thus, the idea that scholars simply cannot be sure of the dating of certain texts often proves difficult for students to grasp. Erin consulted a variety of sources to get some sense of the issues behind dating these traditions, although in the final project there remained some confusion over the dating of sources. Students might be encouraged to sit down with a number of commentaries, preferably reflecting a variety of perspectives, comparing the range of interpretations they offer concerning a text's date, location, authorship, and so on. Most important, because of the nature of Erin's Undergraduate Research program, she had quite a bit of time to spend on her project. She was able to take the time necessary to learn some of the complexities involved with translation and dating texts, unlike the first student I mentioned. She was able to take time to learn to read commentaries and other sources more critically than she did when she started the project, which was a definite accomplishment.

In the end, Erin's project was a successful effort. She completed an article-length discussion of issues related to appropriating ancient myths in modern contexts, which she presented at a regional meeting of the American Academy of Religion, and her work was published in an Undergraduate Research journal, which received positive feedback from reviewers. More important, Erin had completed a project that exposed her to a range of critical issues, which she handled adeptly.

Conclusion

As these case studies reveal, there is a wide range of issues that must be considered when mentoring Undergraduate Research projects in textually based fields. Before the project even starts, it is important to have a clear understanding of the student's language abilities and experiences. A clear assessment of the student's abilities is important as you and the student work together to articulate a project and as you decide how to allot your time. As the project emerges, it is also important to consider whether there are sufficient primary sources in translation for the student to engage. Additionally, one must determine whether or not the student has the time to learn about a range of issues, from the history of textual transmissions to recensions, rhetorical contexts, and so on. While these topics may be broached in introductory courses, understanding and being able to negotiate these issues is something that happens over time. In order for Undergraduate Research in a textually based field to be a successful learning experience, faculty mentors must often help the student researcher frame a project suitable to his or her expertise. This process of framing and conceptualizing the project, especially becoming aware of the limitations inherent to textual studies research that does not use primary language materials, is an important way for students to gain a deeper understanding of the challenges of textual studies research and the skills required to pursue it.

Given the difficulties inherent in textual studies, some may continue to question whether or not the undergraduate researcher whose project uses works in translation can move toward making an "original intellectual or creative contribution" to the field. In spite of these difficulties, it appears that framing a project in a suitable manner helps open up the possibility of moving toward original research. In this vein, those of us working in textually based fields who are committed to offering our students Undergraduate Research experiences need to continue exploring ways of framing Undergraduate Research projects toward this end. One strategy is to encourage students to engage contemporary appropriations of these texts. However, it is important to do so cautiously, as projects often require familiarity with other sets of texts and traditions that bear their own complications and questions. We have to recognize that the complexity of most types of textual study in religious studies means that the student and mentor must work together to craft a project suited to the student's particular expertise and aptitude, which will in turn determine the extent to which the final project may constitute an original contribution to the field. Despite these particular challenges, however, our experiences mentoring these Undergraduate Research projects show that taking on the challenges of textual studies can be extremely valuable and rewarding for students. Undergraduate Research in textual studies provides students an opportunity to hone their skills in critical analysis as well as an opportunity to delve into the complexity of a particular tradition or set of traditions.

Student Reflection on Undergraduate Research

Daniel Webb

My honors project was the first chance I had to really take the time I needed to absorb a wide range of sources. It was a significant challenge to find ways to be more efficient in my research while also opening my ears to listen to a greater diversity of voices and ideas. I think this is the point where I faced the challenge of making an "original" contribution to the field. As I waded through the maze of ideas, trying to bring them into conversation with one another, I had to come to understand where I stood in the midst of it all. In smaller undergraduate projects, one can often get away with simply agreeing with what someone else has said. But when the scope of the project is larger and the sources more diverse, one has to develop his or her own conclusions in order to do justice to all the sources. In this way, the project pushed me to a new level of critical thinking.

NOTES

1. See http://www.lafayette.edu/academics/excel.html.
2. See www.elon.edu/e-web/academics/elon_college/fellows/requirements.xhtml.

PART III

Proposing Standards for Undergraduate Research in Religious Studies

Certainly, the effectiveness of Undergraduate Research in any form is shaped by issues related to the development of the research project. Identifying and executing a research agenda is always situated in the contexts of departmental, institutional, and disciplinary aims, as well as the intellectual development of the student. The chapters in this final section treat each of these contexts respectively.

Undergraduate Research is often part of a student's academic work and can be connected to the major or minor course of study in the discipline. Undergraduate Research is related in a highly intentional way to previous and future course work. Chapter 10 discusses the ways in which faculty mentors play a critical role in working with their students to determine specific learning goals for the research, to develop a research agenda, and to assess the research process and product.

Chapter 11 addresses institutional and disciplinary matters. Undergraduate Research is regularly showcased as a worthy pedagogical enterprise, able to meet well the aims of a liberal arts education. In many cases, faculty and students are assisted in their research efforts by a supporting program, such as a designated office for Undergraduate Research. A cross-sectional presentation of some of the most common existing forms of institutional support draws attention to faculty and student needs and identifies how Undergraduate Research is being recognized as a significant form of teaching in religious studies.

10

Training the Undergraduate Scholar

Nadia M. Lahutsky

"Knock. Knock."

"Come in."

"I was told I could find Dr. Jones here. I am looking for a religion professor to help me with a research project I'm interested in doing."

You are Professor Jones. At this point you:

   a. Adopt a German accent and say, "No Herr Jones here."
   b. Pick up an armful of papers and rush out the door without further comment.
   c. Begin planning revenge on whoever sent this student to you.
   d. Invite the student to have a seat and take a deep breath.

If you were even the slightest bit tempted by any of the first three options presented above, I certainly would not criticize you. After all, you have plenty to keep you busy, what with your class load, publication projects, and service obligations, both to your local institution and to your professional organizations. This current mania to encourage undergraduate students to do research doesn't necessarily seem like a good idea. After all, how many years did it take you in graduate school to master those languages necessary for your doctorate? What twenty-one-year-old has the analytical ability to do serious original research in the area of religious studies? What are the odds that this student will be proposing to work on a topic related to your current long-term publishing project? How seriously will mentoring this student steal time from your own work? Just who was it who sent this student to your door? What was it exactly that the campus vice president for academic affairs said about how he values Undergraduate Research? Will he remember his own words when you give your annual reporting of faculty activity? Indeed, and how many such questions can you entertain mentally while you maintain just the right tone of hospitality and distance in the conversation that is about to take place?

These are all reasonable questions to explore as you consider venturing—or venturing again—into the arena of serving as a mentor to an Undergraduate Research project in religious studies (see chapter 3 for more discussion of mentoring). Given the current state of overly high expectations and relatively low institutional support for most forms of Undergraduate Research, you would be foolish not to ask enough questions to anticipate at least some of the possible problems.

In spite of all the genuine and serious concerns that float through your mind as you stare at the student standing in your office doorway, perhaps you are inclined to invite the student in, not only to avoid rudeness, but because you are not completely opposed to the idea of Undergraduate Research projects. After all, you recall having heard someone say that potential students are increasingly asking if opportunities for Undergraduate Research are evident at your school. You wonder if, perhaps, the very idea of Undergraduate Research in religious studies might attract to your department as majors a few students who have some of the personal characteristics you imagine in an undergraduate researcher. They seem to have more questions than answers as well as an inclination toward being self-motivated learners. You remember the story you heard at the regional meeting about that school down the road that received a hefty sum from a graduate. It seems she had been so shaped by her experience in doing an honors project in that religious studies department that she hoped everyone could be encouraged to do some kind of independent research. Her gift is designated to help support student research projects, honors or not. Besides, you have long argued to anyone who would listen that even your department's best students can't really know if graduate study in the field is for them until they experience personally the hard work, frustrations, and the joys of doing research. Any of these reasons would be sufficient to warrant having a conversation with a student interested in undertaking a research project. Put together, they offer a compelling set of reasons to do so.

Have the initial conversation with that eager student and then give yourself sufficient time to consider carefully whether directing this research project is something you should do. Is the topic in your area of expertise or even close enough to allow you to draw on knowledge and bibliography that you have at hand? Are you interested enough in the area being described to generate the minimum amount of enthusiasm necessary for supervising the project? Maybe the topic is not in your field, but it does represent something you would be glad to be pressed to think more deeply about. Some individuals would never take on a project outside of their specialty; others will. Such decisions may be determined by institutional priorities; for example, if your dean has developed no way to give you credit for taking on projects outside your field, your incentive for doing so is greatly reduced. Perhaps you recently have completed your term on the most time-consuming of all university committees, and you can imagine work on this project fitting into the now-open afternoon. Or, is this the term you have been tapped to chair the search for a new dean? Will you finally have to give in and schedule that hip replacement? An extreme example, maybe, but it would still be relevant data. Decide to take on the project or not, but be clear with yourself and perhaps even with the student about the decisive factors.

Other chapters in this volume consider related issues such as the kinds of research in religious studies that undergraduates might successfully undertake (chapters 5–9, 12), how to frame the methodological considerations of such projects (chapter 4), and how to encourage your own institution to organize for and support such efforts more effectively (chapter 11). This chapter will talk through steps of the process of working with a student engaged in Undergraduate Research, building from the list of best practices as articulated by the Working Group on Undergraduate Research in Religious Studies. It assumes that students undertaking research in religious studies are majors or, perhaps, minors. There may be good reasons to take on a student not in the department, but here they will be assumed to be exceptions to the rule. In many ways, the nature of the process as I envision it is shaped by my own institutional location, a midsized, private, church-related institution in which all students are required to take one course that meets outcomes we have come to call Religious Traditions. Some aspects of the process will vary according to your own institutional location.

Like any good pedagogy, the Undergraduate Research process will vary among faculty members. Nevertheless, there is a developing consensus that successful Undergraduate Research will: build on skills developed in previous course work, develop a research agenda that consists of identifying a research question, propose a methodology appropriate to the question, set forth a tentative time line for completing the steps, and develop a learning contract that includes agreed-upon learning goals for the project. Furthermore, a project proceeds with clear expectations regarding both the relationship between the faculty mentor and the student researcher and how the student grade will be determined. Finally, there should be some specificity to a means of assessment for both the process and the product, and some means should be developed to celebrate both the work product as well as the development of the student as a researcher. Each of these will be discussed in turn below.

Undergraduate Research in Religious Studies Builds on Previous Course Work

The first of these best practices may well be a hard one to meet. Thirty years ago the term paper was a staple of nearly every upper-level course in religious studies. A student took an introductory course, liked it, and took another course in the same department. Soon students were enrolling in courses that began with a "3" or a "4," and that almost always meant they were expected to produce a research paper at the end of the term. There was probably a scramble to accomplish some part of the project, and the completed work definitely required late nights of typing up the final product. Nonetheless, most students did more than one of these papers, and faculty held reasonable expectations that the better students improved in their skills as researchers and sharpened their abilities to write clearly about the topics they had researched. Today these expectations are much less likely to be at all reasonable. Twenty years ago or more the research paper began to go the way of the dodo bird. On my campus I noticed it occurring first in the English department and then spreading through the humanities and social sciences. The arguments against the term paper as an effective classroom assignment all made sense and still do. There was too much work being crammed into a short time. The products seemed to be often cut and paste. Then, increasingly, faculty seemed to catch on to the pervasiveness of term paper mills. In fact, a recent Google search for "term papers" produced over 17 million results. The first thirty hits passed before there was a link to anything not offering for sale high-quality term papers ("not plagiarized"). Weariness set in after viewing the first hundred links, all but a handful dedicated to offering overburdened students a means to solve their assignment needs, including research papers (even dissertations). The law of supply and demand has not yet been suspended, suggesting that there must still be faculty who assign term papers and that may be good news for faculty in religious studies considering taking on a project in Undergraduate Research. In my own department, faculty are split evenly between those who assign term research papers and those who do not. My hunch is that students who have previously purchased term papers are not likely among those who show up at your door asking to do a research project!

Whatever the fate of term papers in your department, you will need to determine what experience your hopeful researcher has had in undertaking research. Use direct questions and ask to see work products. "What courses have you had thus far in the major? What assignments have you completed that engaged you in critical reading and thinking? Talk to me about how you generally go about developing a thesis for a paper. What did you learn about yourself in the process? What did you learn about the study of religion? What topics have you researched? How did you deepen your capacity to access library resources? May I see the final written product? How would you determine it could have been stronger? What kinds of questions did you learn to ask?" A cluster of questions like this will energize the serious student as researcher; it will have an opposite effect on the student who was simply making a casual inquiry! Surely our job is not to scare off students interested in engaging the field that we ourselves love. Nonetheless, we owe to the student in question— as well as to ourselves—an honest laying out of the preconditions that lead most often to a successful project.

The Process Includes Developing a Research Agenda

If the student who sought you out to talk about doing a research project still remains interested after you have gone through the list of probing questions, you may be on your way to mentoring an undergraduate student doing research in religious studies. The first major task looming before the student is to identify a research question.

Developing a research question presupposes that the student has identified a subject of interest and is in the midst of reading widely around the subject. As faculty mentor, you deserve to have available to you all the relevant information concerning a student's progress. Develop some system of information sharing that works for both of you. In addition to face-to-face meetings, this could be a set of ongoing email exchanges or developing a web-based component for the project on eCollege or Blackboard. The latter could be set up to allow for electronic exchange of bibliography and webliography and as a site for dropping off drafts to be read for response. Don't create structures for their own sake. If it's helpful, use it. If not, develop what will work to keep your student and you on track.

Now is the appropriate time to press and prod the student to take the broad topic that has been the subject of much reading and begin to identify a research question. This is a crucial stage, for without this narrowing process, the project will sprawl beyond all manageability and both you and your student will find retaking control an imposing task. If you don't develop the research question at this relatively early stage, the student will keep reading (not in itself necessarily a bad thing!). Without tightening the focus insufficient time may remain for the student to do a good job with the writing.

Making the move from "an interest in the Catholic church and the arts" to "the interior design of local parishes, one built in 1950 to one built in 1999" marks a shift from a broad question to a narrower focus and this ability to focus should yield an even tighter question, such as: "What are the representations of Mary in each place and how can I explain the differences?" Likewise a student may go from a general interest in the role of women in new religious movements to asking why women are attracted to the Church of Scientology. Reaching the point of developing the research question can only occur when the student has done enough reading to see the distinctive issues residing within the larger topic and the faculty mentor has asked enough questions to see the student's face light up with interest. Those sparkling eyes will be a clue to the more narrow topic that should be explored, and your pointed questioning can lead to the development of a question that will guide the remainder of a student's work, at least until such time as the additional research entails the further refinement or even refocusing of the question.

The Process Includes Developing a Research Method

Embedded in the process of identifying a research question will be the development of a methodology appropriate to the question. This area is perhaps the locus of the most profound difference between mentoring an undergraduate student and a graduate student. If, for example, a graduate student enters a master's-level program in religious studies intending to pursue a topic in Christian social ethics, the faculty mentor might reasonably expect the student to master both a particular body of knowledge as well as an appropriate research method. The expectations would be even more pronounced at the doctoral level; indeed, the choice of doctoral institutions is likely based on faculty presence and a prior judgment—if only partial—about the type of method to be pursued. But Undergraduate Research is not the same as research done by graduate students. Languages ancient and modern are not likely yet mastered. Undergraduates pursuing majors in religious studies are acquiring knowledge about the various subtopics within the field, but they may remain fuzzy about the different methodologies. The faculty mentor working with an undergraduate student has the responsibility to help shape the research question and the methodology so that two elements are taken into consideration. The first element is the nature of the question being developed and the second is the existing skill set of the student researcher; yet a third element is the time available to the project.

The student wishing to investigate design elements of local Catholic churches will have to do some reading in art and architecture (to develop a sufficient vocabulary to discuss those churches), but the two of you may determine that the project requires thinking historically. Alternatively, if the student's interest turns out not to be historical but more about types of devotion, that student may need to master the skills of visual analysis and some of the literature in viewer-response criticism. The information needed to determine in which direction the project will go may emerge only after a few conversations with the student. Additionally, if yours is a department in which fewer than half of your colleagues are likely to assign a research paper in traditional course work, this reality has implications for your student and the question of developing a research agenda. Since the research project being proposed in some way must build on the skills that the student has already demonstrated. You are responsible for asking the questions that will elicit the information you need to determine the next step of the process. Perhaps the student has ample experience developing a précis and then a critical thesis in response to a particular reading. If faculty in your department have encouraged students to visit worshiping communities and write about what they saw, this has led to the development of a skill that can be put to use. A student with only modest experience at writing term papers but who has mastered the art of doing a précis and several site visits has acquired skills that can be employed as the building blocks of a longer research project. Perhaps the student interested in women in Scientology will discover that knowing how to do a précis helps with working through the many official texts but that he or she will also need to develop skills as an interviewer. Is there someplace on campus where this can occur? Does the project duration allow time for mastering another skill, or should the project proceed as an investigation of official texts? Posting and answering questions of this nature will advance the process of choosing a method for the project (see chapter 4 in this volume for further discussion of method).

The Process Includes Setting Forth a Tentative Time Line

Everyone is busy. The one thing in short supply in today's colleges and universities seems to be the time needed to accomplish careful reading and thinking. And yet this is exactly what is required for a student to bring an Undergraduate Research project in religious studies to successful completion.

The only solution to this circumstance is to build the project into everyone's calendar. This may well mean, at least at the beginning of the project's duration, weekly or biweekly office appointments in which the student researcher is held accountable for something, at the very least, an annotated list of readings or activities completed since the last meeting. The annotations would note significant details or perspectives that might be useful in the long run. Students having difficulty narrowing the focus to identify a research question might require a more pointed set of assigned tasks at this stage, to break the mental logjam. Requiring a short response paper to each reading may help the student identify those issues of most interest, accomplishing one more step toward selecting the question that will be the focus for the project. Some faculty report success with students at this stage of a project by having the students keep a reading journal, a self-contained book or notebook in which they record—for their own benefit—their reflections on readings. This notebook becomes a kind of private space in which both brilliance and banality might be recorded. Such informal writing can reacquaint a student with the joys of reading, a pleasure often lost in the overly scheduled world of university life today, and it can jog the mind in ways that may not happen in the course of doing more formal writing. The personal journal writing would surely be the basis for the more formal reports that the student brings to regular meetings with you.

Indeed, before a project is too far along, the faculty director and student researcher absolutely must develop a learning contract. An effective learning contract would contain a number of blank spaces. Both parties would contribute elements to the contract, but it should contain—at the very least—the dates of regular meetings between faculty and student, a statement of the research question (as early as it can be formulated), a description of the research methodology (as it is developed), and various due dates for parts of the work product. As the research question gets refined and new avenues of inquiry open up, the blank spaces in the contract can be filled in and some of the earlier elements revised. A sample contract—"Undergraduate Research Project Learning Contract"—is included in this volume (see Appendix II).

In addition to setting frequent and regular accountability sessions, the faculty mentor will need to work with the student to establish other elements of the time frame for completing the project. Frequently the final due date for a project is set by institutional realities. If the research is for a senior thesis, then that date is likely set in stone. Likewise, if the project will be leading toward a public presentation at one's local institution, the day is not open for negotiation. Or maybe your student will be presenting at a regional professional meeting or the Council on Undergraduate Research (CUR) meeting. Those events would serve as a distant target.

The time between the onset of the project and that distant target needs to be managed. Even the brightest and most diligent of undergraduate students will benefit from some intermediate due dates. Establishing an expectation that very early on the student will write up a subsection of the research can be valuable for getting the student out of the reading mode and into the writing mode. Even if substantial portions will later need to be rewritten, this will not have been wasted effort, especially if it helps the student in the process of formulating the thesis that will eventually govern the final written work.

That period of time between developing the research question and the presentation of a first draft will seem to the student—at the beginning of the project—vast, maybe even unlimited. However, the experienced faculty mentor knows that it can evaporate like raindrops on a hot sidewalk. The faculty mentor can help here by treating each of those weekly or biweekly accountability sessions as a sacred trust. While the student may, on occasion, ask to cancel for lack of progress, the faculty partner should let nothing interfere with this appointment. Even if the progress seems slight, it gets honored and factored into the emerging whole; and keeping the scheduled appointment might turn out to help the student identify obstacles that have been hindering progress. At this stage, the faculty mentor assumes the role of sage guide. Act as though any particular appointment isn't all that important and the student may move into a dallying posture and every other class assignment or student organization responsibility may get priority over this research project. But being completely inflexible has its own set of problems. The student will never learn to rely on her own internal motivation for the work if she begins to feel she is simply meeting your schedule. You will have to decide how much you can bend on some of these mini-deadlines, and the answer should have more to do with what you have come to understand as the needs of your student rather than your own personal work patterns.

Because of the interdisciplinary or multidisciplinary nature of the study of religion, most student projects will overlap with the work of at least one other professor on your campus, in history, sociology, literature, psychology, or any other relevant department. When the student researcher is sufficiently engaged with the material to feel confident about it, encourage the student to initiate a few conversations. Provide the appropriate nudge, if necessary. You may have to coach your student through the first few lines of such a conversation. However, the chances are good that a colleague in another department will genuinely welcome a brief discussion with an informed student about a topic of mutual interest. In any case, you are likely to know which individuals on your campus have a reputation for being too busy for such conversations. Direct your student researcher to other professors.

Deadlines, Deadlines, Deadlines

If the Undergraduate Research project is for a grade, you may be able to identify that absolutely final, drop-dead deadline for you as faculty mentor and evaluator to turn in a grade for the project. You will want to be fair to yourself and to your student and allow sufficient time for you to give your final reading and assessment of the final product. Counting back days or weeks from that date would give the project deadline to the student researcher. Every experienced writer knows that one final deadline is not sufficient. You will want to build into the project time line intermediate deadlines. Just past the halfway point would be an excellent time for the student researcher to write up a preliminary report to submit to you. A helpful report would include discussion of materials consulted and other kinds of research completed, a narrative of anticipated research yet to be done, and a tentative time line for the remainder of the project time. Such a time line would necessarily include one or more dates by which you would receive a draft of all or part of the written product. You might want to negotiate these dates with the student, but this would certainly be an appropriate time to exercise a little toughness in regard to deadlines. No students doing long-term research projects should imagine that their project advisors will be staying up late reading their final product. Pressing students, where necessary, to embrace high standards of professional behavior in this regard will benefit both of you. Furthermore, setting early on in the process those high standards for meeting deadlines will help avoid potential misunderstandings and hard feelings as the project nears completion at the same time the term is coming to an end. Certainly, setting early dates can allow space for the inevitable interruptions and bouts of writer's block.

Those early dates can help with another crucial aspect of a research project—successive rewrites that continually improve the final result. Assuming that the work product is a paper, the supervising professor cannot stress too much the necessity of multiple revisions. Setting out the expectation for these multiple revisions and building in the time for completing them must be matched by an obvious professorial willingness to respond to the drafts. Good students appreciate the value of this kind of mentoring to their intellectual development and the contribution to the final product will be invaluable.[1]

Learning Goals

You and your student will need to include in the contract for the project some consideration of learning goals. At the beginning stages, this may seem a bit odd, especially to the student. After all, isn't this obvious? The student wants to learn more about the topic chosen and wants to produce whatever you two agree should be the result (the completed honors project or senior thesis, a research paper, a video, etc.). You, as the experienced mentor in this process, know better than to confuse completely the final work product, important though that is, with broader learning goals. Thus you will draw from your experience in mentoring previous projects to produce a list of possible learning goals, all of which you have seen emerge from Undergraduate Research projects.

Below is a list, helpful but hardly exhaustive, of learning goals appropriate to consider (See chapter 1 for additional learning goals). At the completion of an Undergraduate Research project in religious studies, a student should be able to articulate some of the ways in which he or she has seen the following goals met:

- Contributing to knowledge in the field;
- Cultivating the ability to exercise analytical, critical, and creative thinking and improving one's ability to share the results of that thinking, in both written and oral formats;
- Offering the opportunity for serious active learning that allows for integration of knowledge simultaneous with the chance for more meaningful interaction with a faculty member;
- Learning and demonstrating resourcefulness in overcoming obstacles (research, analytical, personal) that may emerge in the course of the project;
- Stimulating an interest in pursuing research in the field or—perhaps more realistically for most students—exploring to what extent research in the field of religious studies is vocationally meaningful for them by providing a window on the intellectual life of the scholar;
- Experiencing the joys and frustrations of intellectual discovery.

There may well be other learning goals that you and your student would add to a particular project. Resist the temptation to go overboard in identifying learning goals at the onset of the project. Many students would be aided by going over a list of learning goals, such as this one, in conversation with a supervising professor. Student and faculty mentor should discuss the learning goals, think about them independently for a brief while, and then come back together to reach an agreement on which should be considered primary learning goals and which will be of secondary importance for this project. At roughly the middle of the project (defined either by the amount of time before a completion deadline or the number of tasks completed), the list of learning goals should be revisited and numbers reassigned.

Mentoring the Undergraduate Student Engaged in a Research Project

In addition to the student having sufficient background to carry out a research project and the determination of a research method appropriate to the subject, perhaps no other element is so crucial to the success of an Undergraduate Research project than the quality of mentoring that the faculty advisor provides (See chapter 3 for additional discussion of mentoring). Mentoring may also be among the most complicated of factors affecting any Undergraduate Research project. Unlike dealing with a student in one of your regular courses, the faculty mentor of an undergraduate engaged in a research project must recognize that the two of you are working without a syllabus. The level of control an instructor has over a term-long course is considerably greater than that which a mentor has over the execution of a research project. After all, if a bad-weather day forces a disruption in the class schedule, you, as the instructor, can simply adjust the calendar as needed. A research project, however, must be carried out to its conclusion, and no one can tell precisely where that is until it is in sight. Effective mentoring can make the difference between a project merely completed and one whose completion also signals significant intellectual and personal growth on the part of the student and a genuine sense of satisfaction for the faculty mentor.

While the specific details of the mentor-mentee relationship will undoubtedly have to reflect the realities of any particular institutional setting and the personalities of the professor and the student researcher, there may be some elements that all or most would include. Certainly both the faculty mentor and the student mentee will need to engage in both self-reflection and conversation with each other in order to be clear about motivations for and expectations of the effort together. These could be written into the project contract, just to be certain that both parties remain clear about them.

At the early stages of a research project, the mentor may well be quite directive about any number of issues, including which books or articles need to be read first and how to keep track of information. The mentor may also be the one asking the greater number of questions during any of the regular meetings and setting out the priorities for the next one. The mentor may push hard to assure that early deadlines are met. The mentor is, after all, more experienced in such matters, having completed any number of research projects of her own as well as having mentored student projects through to success (or perhaps even disaster). Not to use one's own experiences to benefit a current student engaged in a project can be seen as irresponsible. However, if a project is moving smoothly and the student researcher is demonstrating an ability to engage successfully in the steps of the project, the mentor rightfully employs a less intrusive hand, as seems appropriate. The faculty mentor cannot simply be a calendar-keeper, enforcing deadlines as one might with a syllabus. Rather, faculty have to decide when the long-term needs of the project are best met by relaxing a deadline and, just as important, when doing so would be detrimental to the successful completion of the effort. Thus, the faculty mentor has to be willing to think about this, and—to think smartly about it—the faculty mentor has to know how the project has been developing. In short, the faculty mentor has to remain engaged without usurping ownership of the project from the student.

An effective mentor can help an average student do a good Undergraduate Research project and a good student do a great one. This would be accomplished by drawing the best out of each student and helping each one both to make good use of already identified strengths and to grow in those other areas necessary for the project. Indeed, some research suggests that undergraduate research projects in which students worked with an engaged faculty mentor led to improved outcomes, especially for students in groups historically underrepresented in particular disciplines.[2] Higher graduation rates and a greater likelihood of students pursuing a second degree in their field are demonstrated outcomes of Undergraduate Research and are good reasons to encourage faculty to mentor students in research projects.[3]

Nonetheless, all students can benefit from the close working relationship with a faculty member in their department. A strong correlation between Undergraduate Research experiences and alumni satisfaction and success has been shown in at least one study.[4] The research experience can transform a major's experience in an undergraduate department into a memorable one.[5]

The intended outcomes of increased learning and more future success would, presumably, be even greater the closer the mentoring relationship approximates that of two colleagues working on a common task. Institutional understandings of Undergraduate Research sometimes presume a more genuinely collaborative working relationship and end product than has been the one imagined in this discussion. In such situations, a project may lead to a coauthored paper accepted for publication, increasing the satisfaction level for both student and professor alike. Our colleagues in the natural sciences are quite familiar with the process of including the name of an undergraduate student as one of the coauthors of a publication. The phenomenon is much less common in the field of religious studies in which jointly authored publications, in general, are not the norm and an undergraduate student's contributions to one's own work is likely more properly honored in an appreciative footnote.

Nonetheless, every successful Undergraduate Research project included a faculty mentor who managed to identify appropriate boundaries. Such boundaries facilitated the close professor-student working relationship that was a necessary part of completing the research. The boundaries also would help the mentoring relationship not become one in which the student relies too heavily on the mentor's judgment, never developing the self-confidence necessary for truly independent work. Additionally, maintaining appropriate boundaries for the mentoring relationship will help assure that the working relationship never becomes an emotional or sexual relationship, destined to harm and not help our students.

Assessment of the Project

Like it or not, assessment is a fact of life in the contemporary academy. If faculty in religious studies hope to receive full institutional credit for the work done mentoring Undergraduate Research projects, then we simply must develop, execute, and file assessment plans and data that demonstrate those efforts. Otherwise, this work will remain invisible to those who manage institutional budgets. Thus, the departmental assessment committee (or its equivalent) should be asked to develop an Undergraduate Research project assessment instrument that is the absolutely simplest one that can get the job done. You will need to follow the particular advice of your own college or university's assessment office. However, the following paragraphs offer some advice to that departmental committee charged to create some structure for assessing projects in your religious studies department.

Assessment of Undergraduate Research in religious studies at the departmental level will necessarily involve qualitative methods. Each faculty mentor must be required to complete the assessment process at the end of a project. The most difficult element here will be the faculty tendency to see turning in the grade as the end of his or her responsibilities. Overcome this and assessment will practically take care of itself! Provide both the form and a clear indication of where the completed forms should go and you may well find that assessing Undergraduate Research projects will become the lightest portion of your assessment load.

The form should ask for narrative descriptions of how well the learning goals were articulated and to what extent they were met during the course of the project. Likewise, the assessment of each project should include attention to the learning contract and how effectively it helped guide both student and mentor through the process. The student researcher and the faculty mentor should each provide a one-page narrative self-assessment of their own efforts along the way. Finally, an evaluation of the work product itself will be included as a part of the assessment, with attention to the strengths and weaknesses of the completed work, whether it is a paper or some nontraditional form. Privacy issues may require the grade itself be suppressed.

Ideally, the completed assessment narrative for each project will be collected in an accessible place such as a department common drive, blackboard site, or old-fashioned filing cabinet. By collecting all of these narrative reports, the department chair or the faculty member responsible for assessment can easily produce a report on your department's efforts in regard to Undergraduate Research. Such information can be quite useful in describing departmental workloads, especially if your institution does not have a centralized Undergraduate Research office that would already be collecting data on the projects. Skip this step and the work of mentoring an undergraduate student in a research project may well become nearly invisible, something that is not likely to benefit the faculty mentor, your department, or your students.

Public Dissemination of Research Results

Once you and your student see that both of you have survived the project, please resist the temptation to rest too soon! Your own as well as your student's satisfaction will be increased if you and your department develop the expectation that all students who complete an Undergraduate Research project will share their work publicly. The range of opportunities is wide: an intradepartmental seminar to which are invited all faculty and majors, college or campus honors presentations, regional professional society sessions, CUR conferences, and so on. The completed paper may be quite long. An oral presentation of it may be quite brief, forcing the student to yet another exercise in critical thinking to determine how best to present the heart of the findings. You may judge that the final product presents findings significant enough to warrant even wider distribution; that would be the time to help the student prepare the paper to be submitted for publication.

Whether the paper is eventually published or not, the completion of the project is a time for celebration. You have contributed to a particular student's experience of deeply engaged learning.[6] On even a gloomy day, you can take heart that you have participated in what many of us would identify as the most satisfying of all forms of professor-student interaction and you may never again be tempted to work on your fake German accent.

Student Reflection on Familiarity with a Discipline

Daniel Webb

In general, I think it takes at least a full academic year of research to study a subject with the level of depth that can be transformative. When I compare my honors project with my senior paper (which is generally the capstone project at my institution), the latter seems extremely shallow. The honors project, however, required a real commitment to the research process and a significant personal investment in the subject matter. Prior to my project, I honestly was not especially interested in church-related colleges and universities (my professor suggested the topic). By the end of it, however, I cared a great deal about the subject and felt much more invested in the past, present, and future of my institution. It also probably had some influence on my decision to explore secondary education as a vocation. In my opinion, intensive Undergraduate Research often enables students to find the happy medium between just "doing the work" and burning out from overexposure to a narrow subject. This is the space where the passion of young people can truly blossom.

NOTES

1. Richard J. Light, *Making the Most of College* (Cambridge: Harvard University Press, 2001), 58–62.

2. B. A. Nagda, "Undergraduate Student-Faculty Research Partnerships Affect Student Retention," *Review of Higher Education* 22 (1998): 70–72.

3. E. Nnadozie, J. Ishiyama, and J. Chon, "Undergraduate Research Internships and Graduate School Success," *Journal of College Student Development* 42 (2001): 145.

4. Karen W. Bauer and Joan S. Bennett, "Alumni Perceptions Used to Assess Undergraduate Research Experience," *Journal of Higher Education* 74 (2003): 210–212.

5. Light, 81–97.

6. David Lopatto, "Undergraduate Research as a Catalyst for Liberal Learning," *Peer Review* 8, no.1 (Winter 2006): 22.

II

Promoting Institutional Support

Mark Gstohl

Upon completion of my third-year review at Xavier University of Louisiana, a historically black and Catholic university, I received a letter from the Rank and Tenure Committee that outlined areas that I needed to address. As part of the review, the committee encouraged me to engage in short-term research projects that could also involve students. I was excited about this suggestion because I enjoy serving as a mentor in Undergraduate Research and value this pursuit as a means of preparing our students for graduate studies.

I immediately took advantage of a grant opportunity from our Center for Undergraduate Research to engage in Undergraduate Research with two of our theology majors. Since both students were scheduled to be enrolled in my fall course on modern theology, I invited them to develop papers that could be submitted to the regional meeting of the American Academy of Religion in the following spring. They were excited for the opportunity to begin the projects for several reasons. Certainly, they were thankful for the stipend they would receive, but of equal importance was the opportunity to present their work at a regional conference. Finally, they hoped that their projects could be used as their capstone papers.

Quite frankly, had I not been encouraged by the Rank and Tenure Committee to do so, I probably would not have sought out my students for the project. In order for the project to be helpful to the students and acceptable as a panel presentation at a regional meeting, the research had to extend beyond the fall course work.

Although the additional research required of the students would benefit them as it contributed to their capstone course, the project would not advance my research. Thus, the additional time spent with the students over the course of the spring semester, while personally rewarding, was certainly time that I was not spending on my own research agenda. While the small stipend that I received was appreciated and the grant money would enable our travel to the conference, the most important factor justifying the investment of my own time and energy was the fact that I knew the work was supported by Xavier's administration and was valuable in my tenure process. The experience was a great success! The institutional support I received allowed me to dedicate the time necessary to help the students develop their papers, and we presented a panel discussion at Xavier in the spring of the following year. Not only was the process of helping students develop their research and communication skills rewarding, but also I knew that my work as a mentor was valued by the university.

Identifying Barriers to Undergraduate Research

The support that I received at Xavier is not necessarily normative. V. Daniel Rogers described the current state of Undergraduate Research in the humanities thusly: "models for including undergraduates in research in the humanities are few, funding at many institutions is scarce, and the value of such research in promotion and tenure decisions is often ill defined."[1] Rogers is right. In order for Undergraduate Research in religious studies to flourish, students and faculty must receive support from their departments, their institutions, and the academy. Unfortunately, the support that I received for working with students on Undergraduate Research projects is not available to every religious studies faculty. In a recent article, Mitchell Malachowski reported several barriers for faculty when engaging in mentoring Undergraduate Research including a departmental and disciplinary culture that does not encourage Undergraduate Research, a lack of institutional commitment, compensation and resources insufficient to support and promote Undergraduate Research, and a belief that undergraduates are unable to engage in meaningful Undergraduate Research.[2] These four issues represent significant challenges for institutions and faculty who are interested in promoting Undergraduate Research on their campuses. While other chapters in this book have focused on the issue of student preparedness for Undergraduate Research (see chapters 2, 4, and 10), this chapter will provide a summary of existing institutional mechanisms for supporting Undergraduate Research, discuss student and faculty needs, identify Undergraduate Research as a significant form of teaching, and suggest some "best practices" used by institutions and departments in support of Undergraduate Research in religious studies.

In addition to the common barriers identified by Malachowski, faculty in the humanities face an additional set of struggles as we think about how to explore and expand a pedagogical practice that emerged out of the natural sciences into fields of study that are not necessarily field based or laboratory based. David Bost identified several obstacles to Undergraduate Research in the humanities including students' lack of abilities to conduct research and the nature of humanities research as time consuming and solitary in character.[3] While these objections are common complaints for faculty in the humanities, they must be overcome because of the numerous benefits of introducing students to research. Reed Wilson argues that the mentoring process in the humanities is fundamentally different from the way the sciences go about doing Undergraduate Research. He maintains that "administrators must recognize that, in our field, mentoring is always a time-consuming teaching activity often unrelated to specific faculty research projects." Thus, Undergraduate Research in the humanities must be "backed up by real structures that at the very least account for mentoring as a part of faculty courseload."[4]

Existing Practices

Because so little research has been done on Undergraduate Research in religious studies, faculty members may not be aware of the resources or strategies used in institutions and other disciplines to promote Undergraduate Research. In what follows, I will offer examples of existing practices that can serve as a means of introducing religious studies faculty to successful Undergraduate Research programs at various types of institutions.

The first Undergraduate Research program in the country was the Undergraduate Research Opportunities Program (UROP) at MIT in 1969. More than 45 percent of MIT's faculty participate in the UROP program each year and about 80 percent of the undergraduates engage in a project before they graduate. Students are encouraged either to design their own Undergraduate Research projects and seek a faculty advisor or to join an established faculty member's research project. Students can engage in research throughout the school year or during the summer. Student buy-in to Undergraduate Research at MIT is so strong that some students participate in the program without remuneration or course credit. During the "independent activities period" in

January of each year, student mentors help prepare other students to do research.[5]

Another successful program is the EUREKA model developed at the University of Texas at Austin. The program has several components designed to encourage student and faculty participation in Undergraduate Research. For students, the EUREKA program provides centralized research advising that helps students connect with faculty projects and a web-based database that lists faculty projects in which undergraduates can participate. The program also introduces students to faculty engaged in research by means of one-credit inter-disciplinary seminars for freshmen and sophomores. In these courses, students are exposed to the variety of projects in which the faculty at UT Austin are engaged. Faculty participation is encouraged and rewarded in several ways. The Provost's Office honors faculty engaged in Undergraduate Research with a reception each year. It also "provides matching funds to support faculty research in departments where students win undergraduate-research awards."[6] Faculty must also provide a summary of their experience with Undergraduate Research on their annual faculty report.

Other successful programs exist throughout the country. Many of these programs engage in similar activities, and so there is some value in examining how some of these are addressing the needs of students and faculty in religious studies.

Meeting Students' Needs

Undergraduate Research can be an important part of a student's course of study, although there may be challenges for some students as they try to locate a place for it in their academic program.[7] Research has demonstrated that students who are involved in Undergraduate Research early in their academic careers are more likely to matriculate and attend graduate school.[8] While it is certainly true that some students have no difficulties arranging Undergraduate Research opportunities, a number of students, especially underserved students, may encounter significant barriers to finding the time to devote to research beyond the classroom, for example, during the summer months. Thus, institutions should consider carefully whether they need to provide some form of remuneration for students engaging in Undergraduate Research, especially when it occurs in these contexts, and provide course credit for their work so that all students will have broader opportunities to take part in Undergraduate Research. I have been fortunate that the projects in which my students and I have been engaged have included funding for the students since all of the projects have originated from course work, but have extended beyond the course into either the next semester or into the summer.[9]

Another strategy to meet the needs of students is to make library resources more accessible to them. At the University of Rochester, researchers discovered that the hours of operation at the university library needed to be expanded in order to accommodate students engaged in Undergraduate Research. The library developed a "Night Owl Librarians" program to meet the needs of students who, because they worked after school, could only utilize the library late in the evenings and on weekends.[10] Libraries could offer additional support in the form of carrels, discounts on printing fees, free Interlibrary Loan privileges, or offering classes or workshops on library research. In the freshman seminar that I teach at Xavier, I regularly invite a librarian to teach sessions on research. In addition to introducing students to the various resources available to them, the librarians also address such topics as how to evaluate resources to be used in research and how to avoid plagiarism. The sessions are usually conducted by our Reference Outreach Librarian who provides students with his e-mail address and extension number so that they will have a contact person at the library. This is especially helpful because some of our freshmen are hesitant to ask for help in the library.

One of the problems of doing Undergraduate Research in religious studies is that some of our projects require more than one semester of research. One of the students I mentored in an Undergraduate Research project funded by our CUR program for one semester was not satisfied with the results of her research and wanted to do further study. She applied for and received funds from our McNair program, a program designed to increase the numbers of first-generation, low-income, and underrepresented students completing doctoral programs, so that she could continue her research. The program provided on-campus housing for the student as we worked on the project throughout the summer. In this instance, the student took the initiative to seek an additional source of funding so that she could expand her Undergraduate Research project. A similar approach was used by the University of the District of Columbia (UDC). In order to expand the number of students receiving financial support for Undergraduate Research, the university leveraged connections between various programs. UDC students and faculty not only rely on university-established programs to fund Undergraduate Research but also seek support from external research programs such as National Science Foundation (NSF) and National Institute of Health (NIH) programs to support their Undergraduate Research.[11] These kinds of programs and supports are essential for the successful support of potentially marginalized students in our institutions who may not have the economic resources that enable them to take advantage of traditional Undergraduate Research opportunities.

In addition to financial support, institutions can provide an "incentive" to the student in the form of providing the student with an opportunity to publish the results of the research in a peer-reviewed journal. A recent publication by CUR listed over forty journals dedicated to publishing work by undergraduates.[12] Laurie Grobman recounted how she and a colleague were so inspired by the fact that four of her students published their work in *The Oswald Review* that they started their own undergraduate journal.[13] Undergraduate journals can prove particularly helpful when they employ student reviewers.[14] Xavier University also has a journal for highlighting Undergraduate Research. While XULAneXUS is not a student-led journal, students are involved in the review process and serve with a faculty mentor on the review board. Student reviewers gain a new insight into the research process as they work alongside faculty in their field of study critiquing and evaluating research submissions. My work as a faculty reviewer/mentor proved very rewarding because I mentored one of my theology majors in the review process. I also encouraged him to submit a work to the journal that was published in the next issue. I was so impressed by this work that I helped him submit the paper to a regional meeting of the American Academy of Religion. The paper was accepted, and I was able to secure funding for him and accompany him to the conference.

Another way to encourage undergraduates to pursue research opportunities is to showcase their research in a symposium. A symposium provides many benefits to students, faculty, and the university. Students engaged in Undergraduate Research can make public their endeavors while students who have not had an opportunity to do research can begin dialogues with students and faculty engaged in Undergraduate Research and perhaps begin projects or join ongoing projects. Faculty may also connect with faculty from other disciplines engaged in similar pursuits and begin collaborative projects that can also include students. Carolyn Ash Merkel pointed out that the Undergraduate Research Symposium at the University of Washington provides students, faculty, and the community with the opportunity "to discuss cutting-edge research topics and to examine the connection between research and education."[15]

Developing a website similar to UT Austin's website that lists faculty research projects is another inexpensive method of encouraging student involvement in Undergraduate Research in religious studies.[16] One of the purposes behind the website is that it "integrates efforts to involve undergraduates in research and efforts to break down barriers to cross-disciplinary study and collaboration."[17] In some cases, students who are not majoring in religious studies may have an interest in a religious studies faculty's research but be unaware of the project. Some students may even have expertise in an area that may enrich a faculty project. For instance, I was asked by a colleague to present a paper on music related to Hurricane Katrina at the session "Music in the Aftermath of Tragedy." I shared this information with several of my classes, and two students approached me about helping identify Hip Hop music related to Katrina. One student is a theology major, but the other student is majoring in biology. He's since changed his minor to theology. As a result of making my research known to students, the presentation will be enriched by undergraduate students. I will seek funding for them through our CUR office, but the students are so excited about the project that they have started their research already. I will rely upon their knowledge of Hip Hop to identify songs that respond to Katrina, and we will work together to identify what themes and concepts emerge so that we can offer a theological critique of the body of work as a whole.

Another means of supporting students is to provide seminars, workshops, or classes focused on research. These types of events can provide instruction for students unfamiliar with the research process and introduce them to the various opportunities for Undergraduate Research in the university. At the University of Colorado at Boulder, the Minority Arts and Sciences Program (MASP) encourages Undergraduate Research by underrepresented students by offering biweekly seminars that provide extra challenge to students enrolled in particular courses.[18]

Several Undergraduate Research programs include a peer mentor component. One suggestion for peer mentoring is to require students engaged in their capstone courses to mentor those who will be beginning the process soon or are in the initial stages of the capstone project.[19] The peer mentors can also provide valuable information that can be used to assess the capstone process as well as to assess how well other courses in the curriculum prepare students for research. At the University of Washington, Undergraduate Research is such a part of the culture of the university that students formed their own organization to promote Undergraduate Research. The Undergraduate Research Society meets regularly to assist students in identifying and applying for research positions. They also present their research and help one another refine their presentations and publications.[20]

Other simple measures can be taken to support Undergraduate Research. Religious studies departments can provide office space and computers for students to engage in research. In the conference room in our department at Xavier, we have encyclopedias, journals, and books available for students to use. We also have bulletin boards that highlight our students' work, and we make sure that when our students publish articles or make presentations that the school newspaper and newsletter are notified.

Faculty Needs

Robert Jacobson identified the phenomenon of "institutional drift" whereby faculty at predominately undergraduate institutions (PUIs) are experiencing more pressure to publish their scholarship than in previous years.[21] However, the same faculty members are also expected to incorporate more student-oriented and time-consuming activities such as service learning and group learning activities and to incorporate technology in the classroom.[22] If faculty at PUIs are under more pressure to publish and Wilson's argument is correct that mentoring Undergraduate Research in the humanities is more time intensive than in the sciences, this might explain why Ronald Dotterer lamented that humanities departments have been the slowest to participate in Undergraduate Research.[23] In fact, a recent study revealed that while student engagement in research-related activities increased between the mid-1990s to 2004, humanities students' engagement actually declined during that period.[24]

Faculty in religious studies are struggling to engage in Undergraduate Research for a variety of reasons. Jeffrey Evanseck et al., point out that heavy teaching assignments, limited funding of students, inadequate access to research facilities and equipment, and a lack of research infrastructure hinder faculty involvement in Undergraduate Research.[25] Additionally, many faculty in religious studies simply have no experience in conducting Undergraduate Research and need help in navigating the process. While this book is one step in helping provide tools to faculty interested in Undergraduate Research, it is also important to encourage discussion concerning the theoretical concerns of Undergraduate Research in religious studies as well as to demonstrate how faculty in various subdisciplines of religious studies have conducted Undergraduate Research. The primary means for encouraging faculty to mentor students through the research process are clear tenure and promotion policies that value Undergraduate Research, workshops and training for persons in religious studies that explore creative ways to conduct Undergraduate Research, administrative and departmental support, curriculum development that incorporates research into course work, and compensation (funding or course releases) for students and faculty engaged in Undergraduate Research.

Having a clear directive from my Rank and Tenure Committee early in my career to recruit and work with students on research projects resulted in my working on two Undergraduate Research projects. Having experienced the personal rewards of these projects, I have continued to seek opportunities to mentor students because of the satisfaction of observing the intellectual growth of my students as they struggled with their projects. Adding Undergraduate

Research as a separate category of the Faculty Annual Report at the University of Texas at Austin has enriched their EUREKA program and has demonstrated to faculty that the university's administration both values and rewards Undergraduate Research.[26]

The Working Group on Undergraduate Research in Religious Studies has also prompted valuable discussion about Undergraduate Research in our field through a set of workshops at national, regional, and local settings; an issue of *Spotlight on Teaching* in *Religious Studies News;* and the present volume. The dialogue between the Working Group members and the persons attending the workshops has been fruitful and provided insight into the value of Undergraduate Research as well as methods of improving Undergraduate Research. As the members continue to share and publish their research, Undergraduate Research in religious studies will expand and improve. However, further support from the academy is needed. In the discipline of psychology, a national study was conducted to evaluate Undergraduate Research experiences in the discipline.[27] This study revealed a need for faculty to integrate Undergraduate Research into required courses and to incorporate more active learning in their courses. A more comprehensive study of Undergraduate Research in religious studies would also be a benefit to our discipline. Funding could be secured through sources related to the discipline itself, through the Wabash Center or the American Academy of Religion or sources related to the humanities, such as the National Endowment for the Humanities (NEH) or through CUR.

From 1993 to 2006, the CUR Chemistry Division had a mentoring network for faculty teaching chemistry.[28] Perhaps CUR could be encouraged to establish a mentoring network for faculty in the humanities or in religious studies. The American Academy of Religion has a variety of venues and services that could be used to promote Undergraduate Research in religious studies. In 2009, the American Academy of Religion conducted workshops on sustainability and leadership. The Academy could be encouraged to offer formal workshops on Undergraduate Research in religious studies. A program unit could also be instituted to address the area of Undergraduate Research. Current resources such as the syllabus project, departmental consulting, summer seminars, awards, or grants could include Undergraduate Research as a component. Theta Alpha Kappa, the national honor society for religious studies and theology, could also be encouraged to seek funds to support students or faculty. It might also be encouraged to develop a faculty award for excellence in promoting Undergraduate Research.

On the departmental level, several strategies can be implemented to encourage faculty participation in Undergraduate Research. Departments can utilize existing funds or seek additional funding from the institution or outside sources for incorporating Undergraduate Research into the curriculum. Since departments regularly engage in program review, in some cases external funds may not be necessary. Departments can also fund faculty memberships in organizations such as the Council on Undergraduate Research (CUR) and the National Conferences on Undergraduate Research (NCUR) as well as pay for faculty to attend conferences and workshops. Faculty members funded by the department can then share the insights gained from these activities with other faculty members. Faculty members who have engaged in Undergraduate Research can serve as mentors for new faculty or faculty wishing to begin a research project. Faculty mentors can also help junior faculty navigate administrative "hurdles" such as the Institutional Review Board (IRB) or grant approval processes.[29] If available, departments can offer release time for faculty serving as mentors to other faculty members or to students.

At the institutional level there are several ways to engage faculty in Undergraduate Research. One way is for universities to sponsor workshops on Undergraduate Research so that faculty can dialogue with others in the discipline who have engaged in Undergraduate Research. In the spring of 2009, Nadia Lahutsky and I presented the workshop "Problems and Possibilities: Engaging Students in Undergraduate Research in the Humanities" to the faculty of Xavier University of Louisiana. The event was sponsored by Xavier's Center for the Advancement of Teaching and Center for Undergraduate Research. Xavier faculty showed most interest in understanding how to incorporate students into their own research and expressed reservations about "using undergraduates as minions." This mind-set demonstrated that some humanities faculty need to be introduced to the benefits of having students engage in the research process. A staff member of Xavier's CUR program that teaches in the area of natural science was present at the workshop and was able to dispel the myth that undergraduates can only engage in menial tasks and that the experience serves only to provide "cheap labor" for the faculty member's research. In fact, Reed Wilson reported that when students were surveyed about their Undergraduate Research experience, they reported that they better understood what research really is and that they learned more in their research project than they could in the classroom.[30]

Professional societies that serve the various disciplines in which religious studies professors engage can also be a valuable resource for expanding Undergraduate Research in religious studies. Members of this Working Group have presented several workshops and presentations for various venues since the group began in 2007, and in each instance, the response of faculty members in the humanities and religious studies has been overwhelmingly positive. In 2007, we shared our experiences as mentors in the Undergraduate Research process with our religious studies colleagues at the national meeting of the American Academy of Religion in a panel discussion entitled "Mentoring Undergraduate Research in Religious Studies." At the 2008 CUR national meeting, several Working Group members led the workshop "Distinctive Epistemologies: Knowing When Student Work Is 'Original' in the Humanities." A cross representation of faculty from the humanities and other disciplines gathered to explore the relationship between how our disciplines view "knowledge" and how that understanding is communicated as "original" content.

Further Suggestions for Support

Obviously providing stipends or other forms of remuneration would encourage more students to engage in Undergraduate Research in religious studies. Since locating such funds is often difficult, especially in the humanities, other means have proven effective for the promotion of Undergraduate Research as a whole and can be employed by persons who value and wish to expand Undergraduate Research in religious studies. Promotion of faculty research via a web-based database has been a successful method for connecting students and faculty at UT Austin. If the institution lacks a means of creating such a system, a faculty member can use her or his own website to promote the research. Simply mentioning the project in courses or announcing the need on a departmental bulletin board can also help spread the word that the faculty member is willing to mentor a student in a project. Encouraging students currently involved in Undergraduate Research to recruit and mentor other students is also an effective strategy for connecting students with faculty.

Offering course credit for Undergraduate Research is another means of rewarding both students and faculty for the time involved in doing research. This can be accomplished through designing a curriculum that introduces students to research early in their program and enables them to develop skills so that they are better prepared to engage in research in the intermediate-level courses. For example, in the history department at Moravian College, students are introduced to the use of primary sources in entry-level courses and are required to use only primary sources when preparing their papers. On the intermediate level, students are required to take a "methods" course so that when they enroll in 300-level courses, the twenty-five-page paper that requires a hypothesis and relies on primary sources is not so daunting a task.[31]

Institutions can support faculty by awarding them with release time to engage in Undergraduate Research because the time requirements for mentoring students in religious studies is significant. Additionally, faculty should be provided with support so that curriculum can be revised to strengthen student research skills throughout their program. Perhaps the most significant means of promoting faculty participation in any activity is by rewarding them with tenure and promotion. By including Undergraduate Research on the annual faculty report at UT Austin, the administration demonstrated a commitment to Undergraduate Research and faculty understood that they were expected to engage in Undergraduate Research and would be rewarded for doing so.

Conclusion

Although institutional support is helpful in encouraging Undergraduate Research, a variety of methods exist for faculty to find creative ways to include students in their research or to help students develop their own projects. Faculty should be encouraged by students who, through their own initiative, seek them out to help them explore concepts or topics more deeply. Working with students as they become excited by new ideas can remind faculty about the joy of discovery and encourage them to a renewed commitment to their own research as well as reminding them of what a privilege it is to be a teacher.

Student Reflection on Public Presentation of Undergraduate Research

Lindsey Hammond

One of the academic significances of this project was being a full collaborative participant in groundbreaking research in religious studies that led to conference presentations and publications. In fact, a highlight of this experience was presenting at an academic conference. As an undergraduate student, it was fascinating to participate in the exchange and discussion of ideas in a formal academic context with faculty as peers. This not only encouraged my pursuit of further graduate studies but also raised my awareness of some of the inner workings of the academy and increased my self-confidence in being able to advance its important work. Additionally, contributing to publications fueled my passion for writing and helped me develop research skills that I have utilized in both academic and church settings.

NOTES

1. V. Daniel Rogers, "Surviving the 'Culture Shock' of Undergraduate Research in the Humanities," *CUR Quarterly* 23, no. 1 (March 2003): 132.

2. Mitchell Malachowski, "A Research-Across-the-Curriculum Movement," *New Directions for Teaching and Learning* 93 (2003): 55.

3. David Bost, "Seven Obstacles to Undergraduate Research in the Humanities," *CUR Newsletter* 13 (1992): 35.

4. Reed Wilson, "Researching 'Undergraduate Research' in the Humanities," *Modern Language Studies* 33, nos.1/2 (Spring 2003): 76.

5. Carolyn Ash Merkel, "Undergraduate Research at the Research Universities," *New Directions for Teaching and Learning* 93 (2003): 49.

6. Paige Schilt and Lucia Albino Gilbert, "Undergraduate Research in the Humanities: Transforming Expectations at a Research University," *CUR Quarterly* 28, no. 94 (Summer 2008): 53.

7. Joyce Kinkead, "Learning Through Inquiry: An Overview of Undergraduate Research," in *Valuing and Supporting Undergraduate Research*, edited by Joyce Kinkead, Special issue, *New Directions for Teaching and Learning* 93 (2003): 6.

8. Karen W. Bauer and Joan S. Bennett, "Alumni Perceptions Used to Assess Undergraduate Research Experience," *Journal of Higher Education* 74, no. 2 (March/April 2003): 223.

9. Philip Hunter, "Undergraduate Research: Winning the Battle for Students Hearts and Minds," *EMBO Reports* 8, no. 8 (2007): 717.

10. Nancy Fried Foster and Susan Gibbons, *Studying Students: The Undergraduate Research Project at the University of Rochester* (Chicago: Association of College and Research Libraries, 2007): 16–19.

11. S. Suzan J. Harkness, Valbona Bejleri, Deepak Kumar, Ahmet Zeytinci, Rachel M. Petty, and Freddie M. Dixon, "Integrating Undergraduate Research Activities into a Campus-Wide Initiative," in *Broadening Participation in Undergraduate Research: Fostering Excellence and Enhancing the Impact*, edited by Mary K. Boyd and Jodi L. Wesemann (Washington DC: Council on Undergraduate Research, 2009), 142.

12. Boyd and Wesemann, *Broadening Participation*, 373–81.

13. Laurie Grobman, "Affirming the Independent Researcher Model: Undergraduate Research in the Humanities," *CUR Quarterly* (2007): 24.

14. Farhan Ali, Nafisa M. Jadavji, Willie Chuin Hong Ong, Kaushal Raj Pandey, Alexander Nikolich Patananan, Harsha Kiran Prabhala, and Christine Hong-Ting Yang, "Supporting Undergraduate Research," *Science* 317 (July 6, 2007): 42.

15. Merkel, "Undergraduate Research," 47.

16. See https://www.utexas.edu/research/eureka/ (accessed March 23, 2011).

17. Lucia Gilbert, Paige E. Schilt, and Sheldon Ekland-Olson, "Integrated Learning and Research Across Disciplinary Boundaries: Engaging Students," *Liberal Education* 91, no. 3 (2005): 46.

18. Alphonse Keasley and Angela Johnson, "Linking into the Academic Network: Supporting Student Success and Program Growth," in *Developing and Sustaining a Research-Supportive Curriculum: A Compendium of Successful Practices*, edited by Kerry

K. Karukstis and Timothy E. Elgren (Washington, DC: Council on Undergraduate Research, 2007): 346.

19. Liz Adams, Mats Daniels, Annegret Goold, Orit Hazzan, Kathy Lynch, and Ian Newman, "Challenges in Teaching Capstone Courses," *SIGCSE Bulletin* 35 (2003): 220.

20. Merkel, "Undergraduate Research," 48.

21. Robert L. Jacobson, "Professors Who Teach More Are Paid Less, Study Finds," *Chronicle of Higher Education* 38, no. 32 (April 15, 1992): 17.

22. Mitchell Malachowski, "A Research-Across-the-Curriculum Movement," *New Directions for Teaching and Learning* 93 (2003): 55.

23. Ronald Dotterer, "Student-Faculty Collaborations, Undergraduate Research, and Collaboration as an Administrative Model," *New Directions for Teaching and Learning* 90 (Summer 2002): 83.

24. Shouping Hu, George D. Kuh, and Joy Gaston Gayles, "Engaging Undergraduate Students in Research Activities: Are Research Universities Doing a Better Job?" *Innovative Higher Education* 32, no. 3 (2007): 171.

25. Jeffrey D. Evanseck, Ellen S. Gawalt, Avivi Huisso, Jeffrey D. Madura, Stacie S. Nunes, Remi R. Oki, David W. Seybert, and Ramaiyer Venkatraman, "Optimizing Research Productivity While Maintaining Educational Excellence: A Collaborative Model," in *Broadening Participation in Undergraduate Research: Fostering Excellence and Enhancing the Impact*, edited by Mary K. Boyd and Jodi L. Wesemann (Washington, DC: Council on Undergraduate Research, 2009): 66.

26. Paige Schilt and Lucia Albino Gilbert, "Undergraduate Research in the Humanities: Transforming Expectations at a Research University," *CUR Quarterly* 28, no. 94 (Summer 2008): 53.

27. Baron Perlman and Lee I. McCann, "Undergraduate Research Experiences in Psychology: A National Study of Courses and Curricula," *Teaching of Psychology* 32, no. 1 (2005): 5–14.

28. Lisa N. Gentile, Nancy S. Mills, and Kerry K. Karukstis, "Faculty Mentoring Faculty: Lending Support Within the Undergraduate Research Community," *Journal of Chemical Education* 83, no. 11 (2006): 1584–86.

29. Elizabeth Thomas and Diane Gillespie, "Weaving Together Undergraduate Research, Mentoring of Junior Faculty, and Assessment: The Case of an Interdisciplinary Program," *Innovative Higher Education* 33, no. 1 (2008): 36.

30. Wilson, "Researching 'Undergraduate Research'," 78.

31. Dennis Glew, "Designing a Research-Driven History Program," in *Developing and Sustaining a Research-Supportive Curriculum: A Compendium of Successful Practices*, edited by Kerry K. Karukstis and Timothy E. Elgren (Washington, DC: Council on Undergraduate Research, 2007): 388–89.

12

Afterword: Mastering Undergraduate Research

Ann Marie Leonard Chilton

[Opportunities for self-reflection during the research process or for future application in later academic work are some of the ways students share their perceptions about the relationship of their research to their own intellectual formation. This information, in turn, can help faculty members as they examine their role in the mentoring relationship and consider further involvement in this pedagogy. For these reasons, a student perspective about the immediate, and long-term, impacts of participation in Undergraduate Research closes this section. – Eds.]

When I chose to attend Elon University in 2001, I was attracted to its smaller size of five thousand students because I knew smaller classes would create better learning environments and less of a distance between students and teachers. I had grown up in a small town in North Carolina and attended a large, public high school where I found it easy to avoid my homework. I wanted to become a better student in college, and I learned from visiting campus that almost all Elon students graduated within four years. In that time frame, many students were able to complete a double major—an idea that appealed to me because I was interested in many subjects, yet I had no idea what kind of work I wanted to do after graduation.

In the course of my sophomore year at Elon, when offered the chance to study independently with a religious studies faculty mentor and do Undergraduate Research, I said yes because I knew I could study a subject long-term and grow in my abilities. Also, with time, my mentor would learn my strengths and weaknesses, and I could learn from her coaching. By the time I graduated, my Undergraduate Research experience had become the most valuable part of my college education, and it equipped me with the skills and confidence I needed for graduate school and life after college.

The First Semesters of College

During my first semester at Elon, I took a few introductory classes in the disciplines that most interested me; then I narrowed my focus and declared a double major in English literature and religious studies. Almost always, I looked forward to writing for literature and religion classes because I knew I could produce a decent paper and would enjoy exploring my thoughts about a particular subject through writing. But my confidence in the value and originality of my ideas and abilities was very low, and I sometimes felt I was barely scraping by in school.

At some point during my sophomore year, a creative writing professor told me I wrote "really bad fiction" and "brilliant essays." But at that time in my life, the only conclusion I was capable of drawing from that conversation was a negative one: I figured there was no place in the "real world" for people who liked to write essays. The message I thought I heard was one that said only fiction writers were real writers, though now I am sure that was not the message my professor meant to convey. Despite reading hundreds of pages of nonfiction articles for English and religious studies classes, I never made the connection that I could think or write in the same way as scholars.

During the second half of my sophomore year, I took the required sophomore seminar that focused on introducing majors to a variety of theoretical and methodological approaches to the study of religions. While the twelve of us all knew we would be expected to write a research paper on a topic of our choosing, we had no idea how we were going to conquer that kind of assignment.

Before this class, I hadn't learned anything about research questions. But in the seminar class, I learned that with a research question I could ask the world what I wanted to know and then work to find an answer on my own. To me, it was a groundbreaking idea that the questions and subjects I was curious about were worthy of formal study in the form of a research project.

I decided to write the research paper on a Christian service community called Carolina Cross Connection (CCC) that I had worked with for four years, and to which I would continue to devote my summer vacations. CCC finds its identity as a community by doing home repairs for the needy in western North

Carolina. I wanted to learn more about the power of community because, from the outside, CCC looked like another outreach ministry, but from the inside, everyone who was committed to its ministry became an exceptionally close group, united by an unseen bond that helped us learn more about ourselves and our place in the world as people who cared about our impoverished neighbors.

So that first paper ignited my interest in exploring the nature of community, specifically religious communities. From my research for the seminar class, I learned that intentional Christian communities are groups of Christians with common beliefs, attitudes, and ways of life who decide to live together, work together, and support one another by living as a group that stands apart from mainstream society. Even though CCC was not an intentional community where people lived year round, I could see the similarities between CCC and intentional communities; this made me want to look into the ways that living in intentional religious community motivates its members to serve the outside world.

When it became clear that I was very interested in learning more, my professor asked me if I'd like to apply to become an Elon College Arts and Humanities Fellow and develop a more extensive Undergraduate Research project that would allow me to explore my research question further. I couldn't believe a professor thought my research paper was worth more exploration, so I was encouraged. Something I had written or said made it clear that I had the ability to become a better student. I appreciate that our classes were small enough and my professors cared enough to notice I had a passion for this topic and to see that my passion could drive my commitment and willingness to do more work.

Layers of Thinking

For me, Undergraduate Research was all about confidence, that is, gaining the confidence I didn't have—and didn't know I needed to have—to venture to the next level in my education. With two years of English and religious studies classes completed, I knew how to formulate a basic thesis and organize my thoughts into a paper; but I didn't know my thoughts were original, important, or even good.

Undergraduate Research was a more intense educational experience because it was a multiyear process, not just a one-semester paper. Devoting two years to a project would certainly yield something of substance that might develop into a book or an even larger project. I wasn't just trying to complete an assignment; I was venturing out on my own and exploring a new path within religious studies.

Working with a mentor helped me develop a larger understanding of my thought processes because the first research paper I wrote during my sophomore year wasn't just another essay to my mentor. She was able to show me how that first paper was a significant step toward a more specific idea. A question burned in my mind, which is why I was interested in the subject in the first place. The research process helped me unearth that question as well as discover some answers. Subsequent papers, or essays, helped me go further down the path of my curiosity and helped me develop a more sophisticated research question that guided my main Undergraduate Research paper. My mentor sat down with me and showed me this process, outlining several different possibilities for the direction of my research. Not only did she teach me how to think; she explained to me that my interests were worth thinking about.

In our seminar class, I had written an exploratory paper and interviewed people who founded CCC, a ministry that had shaped the way I viewed religious faith. That project sparked my interest in intentional Christian communities, especially ones that used their beliefs and energy to serve the poor. The next semester, as part of my work as an Arts and Humanities fellow, my mentor encouraged me to have a wider scope and a less personal one, so I wrote a historical paper during an independent study course. In that study, I researched the phenomenon of intentional Christian communities by examining three influential and historical Christian communities: Benedictine monks in the sixth century, Beguines in the thirteenth century, and Catholic Workers in contemporary society. Finally, I met with a member of the contemporary intentional community and decided I wanted to learn more about his experience as a Catholic Worker.

I kept thinking, throughout this process, about my own summer vacations, which I had spent working in Christian community to serve others. Despite the many positive rewards, the work had been difficult and draining. My mentor assured me that my personal experience was meaningful to what I was learning, so I listened. Soon I figured out what I wanted to know about people who live in community all the time, people who are always serving, giving, and working for change: How do they maintain their lifestyles? From where do they draw their strength and inspiration? How are they sustained?

It was a research question members of the Catholic Worker movement were eager to answer because, they said, outsiders didn't recognize the struggles they faced because of their lifestyle choices. Catholic Workers choose to radically serve the poor and outcast of society by opening their homes to the homeless and vowing their own poverty in order to declare solidarity with the poor. My research examined the spiritual, physical, and emotional exhaustion that Catholic Workers often ultimately feel after giving their lives to the practice of anarchy, pacifism, service, and voluntary poverty, and it pointed out ways Catholic Workers sustained themselves through the challenges inherent in their everyday lives. Finding answers to my research question had the potential to help adherents of any service-oriented religious community understand the importance of finding rest and sustenance while they were giving themselves fully to their ministry work. My research also would offer insight about the direction of contemporary intentional Christian communities.

As I traveled and met Catholic Workers, I learned they often serve time in prison for their radical protests of abortion, the death penalty, weapons, and war. One man I interviewed had recently spent six months in prison because he had chained himself to a weapon that was considered government property. His protest was powerful, yet the cost and consequences were high for him and his family. The Catholic Workers I met knew that because of their lifestyles of protests and "actions," as they called them, they could face really difficult challenges.

Catholic Workers commit to live in constant struggle, standing apart from the world, while, at the same time, embracing and sharing everything they have with the most rejected people of society: homeless people and recovering drug addicts. The more I learned about the Catholic Workers, the more I wanted to learn. Their way of life was very different from anything I had encountered, so they became ideal research subjects for me; I could study their experiences from an objective point of view while, at the same time, I maintained a profound interest in what they had to share.

Having a professor who was willing and able to explore my ideas with me, point me in the right direction, and give me the tools I needed to conduct research is an opportunity that I never would have had in the traditional classroom. Although Elon's class sizes were small and professors knew our names and abilities, which was invaluable, one-on-one attention from a professor in my field was infinitely more constructive because she was able to tell me exactly what kind of work I needed to do in order to create an outstanding project and learn all I could about the subject: I needed to spend hours each week conducting interviews, reading everything I could find, searching for more information, and probing my own thoughts for new paths I could explore within the subject material.

While all my professors at Elon gave interesting assignments, my mentor showed me how to complete the assignments. I had the curiosity and the ability to pursue the information, but I needed someone to give me concrete instruction on how to do the work and do it well.

The Art of Research and Writing

When I wrote my first research paper, my mentor gave me some of the first specific writing advice I received in college: she told me to tell a true story, or an anecdote, to make my introduction more engaging. Even though my first anecdote wasn't thrilling or even well written, I was delighted at the idea that I could tell a true story as part of a paper for school. At that time, I thought essays were formal things; I hadn't discovered great contemporary essayists like David Sedaris, Rebecca Solnit, Gretel Ehrlich, Joan Didion, Annie Dillard, or Wendell Berry. I could not conceive that nonfiction writing was this wonderful, wide genre people had been swimming around in for centuries. But after I wrote my first anecdote, my mind overflowed with true stories I couldn't wait to write down, and my essays for other classes became all the more interesting and multifaceted because now, in my mind, essays could be created, like art, rather than just stated, like instructional pamphlets.

As I was developing my research question, my mentor introduced me to the practice of ethnography. Until then, I didn't know there were different methods of conducting research. I had told her I wanted to interview people to hear their perspectives, so she introduced me to digital voice recorders and helped me apply for a grant so I could buy one. Then she guided me in preparing some questions to ask my research subjects. I was fascinated and even relieved to learn ethnography was a methodology I could use to conduct my research.

After interviewing at least a dozen Catholic Workers about their way of life in an intentional faith community, I spent hours transcribing everything they said. Along the way, I paid attention to their stories and reflections that revealed the most about their experiences, which tended to be spoken in the moments where they were most comfortable and most willing to be transparent about their beliefs. Those great interview moments took place when I had already spent hours with the subjects and had immersed myself in their community life; they were vulnerable moments during which the subjects were speaking truth as they knew it.

The culmination of my Undergraduate Research and interviews would be a forty-page paper. I could tell the paper was going to come together, yet it wouldn't be a clean process. As I looked back at the other papers I had written in preparation for this final project, I could see the improvement in my writing and was amazed at how much writing I had done; it had taken all that practice for me to have the confidence to face the final assignment. I had learned from experience that writers must practice every day, and Undergraduate Research had given me the chance to write more than I ever had imagined possible. Still, the final paper would be written on a clean slate, so I could use the most recent techniques I had learned and express myself clearly as I presented my findings.

As I began to prepare my first draft of that final paper, I gathered hundreds of pieces of data that helped answer my research question. Late one evening, in my senior year, I arranged these "pieces" according to topic and spread them throughout almost every inch of my room: there were newspaper clippings, photocopies, artwork, quotes, transcriptions, notes, highlighted printouts, marked books, and portions of previous papers. My digital recorder had been emptied. The beginnings of something blinked on my computer screen. Then I looked at the pieces I had collected for more than two years and sensed, in some weird way, that I was ingesting it. I *knew* the research material so well, and at that moment, I was sure I could create something really good out of it. It pulsed with meaning. It was waiting for someone to bring it together in a significant way. During this process, I realized research didn't consist of lifeless facts that someone had already discovered and housed in a library. Instead, research was an art, with all the potential for creativity, expression, and philosophy as in any other art form.

I remember that feeling now, when the pieces of *something* are collected. I recognize that sensation; it is the moment midway through creation, when I know the material is going to come together, yet the process won't be as simple as completing a puzzle. Some of the pieces don't belong and will need to go, and some of the pieces need more work. But that moment is when I start working my hardest because I'm in a hurry to preserve the harmony existing among those pieces.

Writing the final paper allowed me, finally, to answer my research question in a satisfying way. Later, I took the forty-page paper and edited it to twelve pages to make it an appropriate length for presentation at Undergraduate Research conferences. Editing the paper further allowed me to better organize the project as a whole. Throughout the process, my mentor had given constructive assignments, such as to create a book outline out of the material. Organizing my research material in long, short, and outlined versions helped me learn more about the organization of ideas. Because of the numerous assignments that led to my final Undergraduate Research paper, the quality of my schoolwork improved in every subject because I was getting consistent practice thinking and writing at a high level.

By far, the most influential part of my experience in Undergraduate Research took place the evening I received the Best Undergraduate Paper award at the Southeastern Commission for the Study of Religion annual conference. The moment they announced my name was an affirmation that my efforts and expression were useful to the academic field of religious studies and, moreover, that my curiosity and interests were legitimate. That award gave me the confidence I needed, especially when I had some discouraging experiences and dead-end jobs after graduation, to say to myself, "I am valuable. My abilities are unique. I have something to offer."

Learning Across the Disciplines

When I remember the fascinating people from the Catholic Worker movement whom I met through my ethnographic research for my Undergraduate Research project, I recall their personalities, their unique beliefs, and their particular place in the world of religious studies. I would never have learned about them in a classroom, because they don't have millions, or even thousands, of followers. And before I met them, I read books for my research that I might never have read in a religious studies classroom: books of training for monastic communities, books of mysticism for women, books of anarchistic essays, and more. Undergraduate Research opened up a world of religious studies I could discover for myself, which made every other college experience richer.

My other classes seemed more meaningful because I began to see the themes of contemporary literature intertwine with theological ideas; I learned more about human nature and different cultures because I noticed commonalities in my interviews, readings, and observations; I could throw away limited points of view that I had been taught and broaden my perspective on issues where I once had thought I knew what I believed, yet I only knew in part.

I learned about the history of the English language while I witnessed the evolution of language in the historical reading I did for Undergraduate Research. My research gave me examples I could use in all my other classes. In the second half of my senior year, my English major required that I write a research paper and present my findings to my classmates in an English Senior Seminar course. After two years of Undergraduate Research, I knew how to shape my interests and readings into a specific research question that would guide my research process.

How can students do good work unless someone shows them how? Writing, studying, researching, reading, interviewing, and public speaking are learned skills that some students will comprehend in the classroom, yet most students will need one-on-one attention to master them. Conducting Undergraduate Research with a mentor will teach students these skills and equip them with confidence as they continue their education.

Two other students my age worked with my mentor at the same time, so the three of us spent nights at the library together, compared notes, called one another, and read one another's papers. We met together with our mentor at least once a week, at first, and then we met less often as we developed clearer goals and direction. We had similar questions: Should I interview more people? Is this story relevant to my research question? Are my findings specific enough? Is this a good book to be reading?

I'm glad Undergraduate Research was a collaborative process because when we met with our mentor, we would update one another on our progress, so it kept us on track with our research hours and gave us a forum to share our ideas and questions. We told one another about our victories with interviews and our frustration with the limited information we found. Then we traveled together to the Duke University Divinity School library to find better material. It was heartening to be able to call one another as we each typed out those final pages of our research papers, and it was nice to know I was not the only student who was completing a large, ongoing assignment in addition to regular assignments from other classes.

As peers, we encouraged one another to call more people, travel to new places, and go further in our efforts to find information. We even competed with one another in small ways, which was a healthy incentive to work as hard as we could. Today we are still good friends because of our shared experiences, and we continue to support one another in our separate graduate school and career endeavors. When we talk or get together, we often recall memories of Undergraduate Research, usually joking that we are not as smart as we once were because we have never had another experience that stretched us so much and required us to do such a large amount of work.

Devotion to the Craft

During the process of researching for and writing my final Undergraduate Research paper, my mentor encouraged me to spend at least ten to twelve hours each week with the material. At the time, that number of hours seemed impossible to spare; but in forcing myself to strive toward that goal, it finally occurred to me how much preparation good work takes. That realization freed me up to throw myself into the research and explore it all the more because I really was interested in it.

Now when I spend weeks or months on the beginnings of a project, I know I am giving it what it deserves. I'm not wasting time; in fact, I'm doing exactly what I should be doing: creating. That discovery, which I made while doing Undergraduate Research, led me to recognize that my interests are valid. I'm interested in certain subjects because of my unique place in the world, and that is no accident. In other words, I might have been placed in a particular situation because I am its ideal storyteller.

In the first research paper I wrote, I had interviewed people who worked in the same ministry as I had, and I was personally interested in what they had to say. But in the context of what I was learning in Undergraduate Research, I could look at those interviews and realize that countless people throughout history had done similar work in their faith communities. My curiosity stemming from a personal experience helped me burn through stacks of books searching for more information on related situations.

Later, as I focused on the Catholic Workers, I could still identify with the people I interviewed. In fact, I was an appropriate researcher for their situation because I was not personally invested in their cause, save for the fact that I knew they had an interesting story to tell that had not yet been told, and I was willing and ready to tell it.

By the end of my senior year, I had presented my paper at three Undergraduate Research conferences and, through that process, gained confidence and public-speaking skills. In one of my jobs after graduation, my manager asked me to present to more than 400 professionals. Instead of being intimidated, I was excited at the opportunity and enjoyed it because I knew I could do it well.

Preparation for Life After College

One of the most invaluable skills I learned in Undergraduate Research was the ability to write thoughtful questions and conduct an interview that would give me substantial research material. I learned I might ask questions for hours and never find anything of substance; but the books, tools, coaching, and editing my mentor provided for me trained me to interview well. I came to understand that whether I agreed with or shared the sentiments of the subjects was unimportant to the interview. My mentor taught me about the distance an interviewer must have from her subject—a professional distance—and this skill became a vital preparation for the workforce as well as for graduate school.

Two years after graduation, I became the principal editor of a website that had more than ten million annual visitors. The website's main content was interviews. The resource for our online articles and information also was taken mainly from interviews. While I had this job, I conducted interviews on the phone, around the United States, as well as in Europe and Latin America. I was relieved to know, when the time came for me to conduct quick interviews with VIPs, that I had insightful questions prepared along with enough confidence in my experience to do my job well.

Because of my Undergraduate Research experience, I took more than a year after graduation to find the ideal graduate program for my skills and interests; I knew choosing the right field and program would be critical. So when I found Queens University of Charlotte's Master of Fine Arts degree in creative nonfiction, I knew it was the right place for me. An edited portion of my Undergraduate Research paper comprised part of my application. The faculty at Queens commented on the diligence and high quality of my work in that paper; yet I had learned those skills through the research process.

My capability and interest in nonfiction writing flourished at Queens University, and I can say with certainty that I would never have found this program or been accepted into it without my Undergraduate Research experience. For my graduate thesis, I presented material I collected through ethnographic research, which continues to be one of my favorite ways to explore the world and find the richness of culture, art, and life.

Because it was the most significant part of my undergraduate education, my experience in Undergraduate Research has fueled all my decisions in regard to the direction of my postgraduate education and career. As a college student, I needed someone to take time with me, train me in thinking critically, affirm my abilities, and critique my unhealthy tendencies so I could move on the next level as an adult, an employee, and a graduate student.

I am grateful for the opportunity to do Undergraduate Research because although I would have graduated from a fantastic school with a solid education, I might never have taken that knowledge far from the classroom. Certainly I never would have gained the ability to connect lessons from everyday life with academics, and I wouldn't possess the confidence, devotion, or passion that I have now in pursuing my graduate studies.

Undergraduate Research as Transformative

As college freshmen at age 18, students often are told they are "adults" and that they have arrived at college because of their hard work in high school.

So when I was taking my first college classes, I thought I was just increasing my knowledge, or adding to an already-existing foundation. However, through the Undergraduate Research process, which challenged me to view a subject from an unbiased perspective rather than through my personal perspective, I could see the educational foundation I had was one made of limited information and basic skills. My educational foundation still needed to be built.

Challenging my own biases and previous knowledge through critical thinking allowed me to read and learn from a different perspective. New information was not a threat to my already-existing views; it was, instead, a chance to stretch my mind around a new level of ideas. For example, in my Introduction to Religious Studies class, which I took fall semester of my sophomore year, I read some feminist theology and felt deterred from anything it had to teach me because, growing up, I had only heard simplistic, negative judgments about feminists. As a child and teenager, I had been exposed to a very black-and-white way of thinking. But when my Undergraduate Research started a semester later, I began to open my mind to ideas that, at first, seemingly clashed with my existing principles. Later, I figured out I was a feminist. But in addition to that realization, I was able to read with new eyes about beliefs and practices other than my own.

When I entered college, I thought I already knew who I was and what I believed, when, in reality, I was a person-in-progress who needed to be stretched and exposed to the diversity of the world, people, cultures, and ideas. When my first semester of Undergraduate Research began, I was able to dig into, appreciate, and understand books and scholarly works about people who held every imaginable point of view about religion, power, relationships, practices, traditions, worldviews, politics, interpretation, and life itself.

The timing of my Undergraduate Research experience, at ages nineteen through twenty-one, was perfect for me because I was ready to start thinking more abstractly and on a wider scope. I was living at a four-year college, the first and last time in my life during which I would be a full-time student immersed daily in an educational environment, so I am grateful my mentor was able to take that opportunity to sharpen my thinking. The amount of work I had to do stretched me as a student and a person. Getting a college education can sometimes seem like a demanding task achieved single-handedly, but having a faculty mentor in Undergraduate Research made my college experience into a challenging journey during which I had a knowledgeable guide.

I think college can be like a rite of passage for those who are fortunate enough to attend. Getting a good college education can make teenagers into educated young adults who will benefit society. For me, the key to that transformation was Undergraduate Research because it took me out of my comfortable, almost predictable, college path and placed me on a journey that would push me to find my own life philosophy as well as my potential as a person and a student.

Student Reflection on Scholarly Community

Erin Keys

Going through the process of Undergraduate Research with other students showed me the intrinsic value of the academic community. To share in the unique experience of Undergraduate Research with scholars your own age creates a dynamic bond. Learning to question, engage, and support your colleagues is an invaluable skill that will benefit all scholars throughout their academic careers and even those who pursue careers outside of the academy. After all, once you graduate and move further into the academic community, your colleagues become the main source of dialogue for your continuing research.

Appendix I: Working Statement on Undergraduate Research in Religious Studies

Religious Studies Statement on Undergraduate Research

The location of Religious Studies within the humanities raises important issues concerning epistemologies, social locations, and student formation and development within Undergraduate Research. The significance of contextual influences upon a student means that one's location within the broader world impacts the questions one raises, the approaches one uses, what one sees as a meaningful research agenda, and the goals and means through which one conducts and evaluates research. Questions and commitments concerning the origins, formation, and validation of knowledge necessarily shape one's interpretation of an "original intellectual or creative contribution" in Religious Studies.[1]

In addition, the multidisciplinary nature of Religious Studies encourages a variety of methodological approaches to the study of religion. Each approach, in turn, provides distinctive understandings of the nature of knowledge, including its recognition, adjudication, appropriation, application, and significance. While all disciplines within the humanities foster attention to how Undergraduate Research shapes the student, the distinctive subject matter of religion connects the student to his/her research in unique ways.

Given these considerations, we recommend that Undergraduate Research in Religious Studies include the following criteria:

I. SELECTIVE. Undergraduate Research is selective insofar as it is most appropriate for those students who have the capacity and the desire to envision, sustain and complete a complex, high quality, and nuanced analysis.

2. COLLABORATIVE. Undergraduate Research is collaborative as faculty and student(s) work together in their formulation of the research project. This collaborative effort represents a unique relationship between faculty and student(s) in which both parties contribute to the research agenda and the final product. The extent of collaboration exists along a continuum. At one end, faculty assign a topic and together with the student(s) cooperate in developing the research process; at the other end, faculty and student(s) are in a collegial relationship in which they work together on a common research project resulting in a co-authored final product.

3. PUBLIC. Undergraduate Research is public insofar as it is of such quality that its public dissemination is warranted and expected. Public dissemination can assume a variety of forms.

4. ORIGINAL INTELLECTUAL OR CREATIVE CONTRIBUTION TO THE DISCIPLINE. The heart of Undergraduate Research centers on the criterion of "an original intellectual or creative contribution to the discipline." "Original intellectual or creative contribution" can be understood as encountering/uncovering new data which are incorporated into existing frameworks, discovering new insights or new data that alter the boundaries and/or contours of the field, drawing novel comparisons or making heretofore unrecognized connections within the field, making new assessments of current knowledge/interpretations based on such standards, creating new visions or interpretive structures that re-integrate/reconfigure what is already known or accepted, applying existing interpretive structures in a new way or in new contexts in order to unfold distinctive integrations/configurations within the field. Some approaches that produce original and creative work within Undergraduate Research in Religious Studies include the following: archival, ethnographic, textual studies, historical studies, cultural studies. The multidisciplinary character of Religious Studies means "original" or "creative" contributions will vary depending on the specific project at hand.

Statement drafted by the members of a Consultation on Mentoring Undergraduate Research (April 2007) and revised by the members of a Working Group on Undergraduate Research in Religious Studies (September 2007).

[1] The Council on Undergraduate Research defines Undergraduate Research (UR) as "an inquiry or investigation conducted by an undergraduate student that makes an original intellectual or creative contribution to the discipline." (http://www.cur.org/about.html)

Appendix II: Learning Contract

[This Learning Contract was developed by Nadia Lahutsky and is intended as a sample that should be modified to reflect specific tasks and learning goals of individual projects. – Eds.]

Undergraduate Research Project Learning Contract

Date: _____

_____   _____

Student   Professor

Project title (tentative):   _____

PART I: DEADLINES OR TARGET DATES (FILL IN OR CHECK, AS APPROPRIATE)

———— Weekly/biweekly meetings (as needed and agreed upon, with clear expectations for what will be discussed at each meeting)

———— Tentative articulation of research question and methodology. State below

———— Revision of research question/methodology, as necessary

———— First written portion due (e.g., history of research, as relevant)

———— First draft due to Supervising Professor for additional review

———— Second draft due to Supervising Professor for additional review

———— Completed project due to Supervising Professor

———— Arrangements made for public presentation of research results

———— Student completes Assessment Form

———— Supervising Professor completes Assessment Form

PART II: LEARNING GOALS

Identify the learning goals most important to project, student, and professor by marking those with "1." The remaining learning goals would, thus, be secondary and should be marked with "2." Student and professor are encouraged to revisit this Learning Goals Contract once around the midpoint of the work and determine if the numbers should remain as originally set.

———— I hope to contribute to the knowledge in the field.
———— I will cultivate the ability to exercise analytical, critical, and creative thinking and will improve my ability to share the results of that thinking, in both written and oral formats.
———— I will experience serious active learning that allows me to integrate knowledge and simultaneously gives me the chance for more meaningful interaction with a faculty member.
———— I will learn and demonstrate resourcefulness in overcoming obstacles (research, analytical, personal) that may emerge in the course of the project.
———— This experience will stimulate an interest in pursuing research in the field and/or help me decide whether research in the field of religious studies makes sense for me by providing me a window on the intellectual life of the scholar.
———— Other (Describe)_____

PART III: EXPECTATIONS

What the student researcher expects from the faculty mentor:

What the faculty mentor expects from the student researcher:

PART IV: UNDERGRADUATE RESEARCH PROJECT ASSESSMENT

Check off as completed and attach the following to this form:
———— Learning Contract
———— Learning Goals Contract (initial and mid-project versions)
———— Professor evaluation of final product (not necessarily the grade)
———— Student self-assessment (one page)
————Supervising Professor self-assessment (one page)

_____   _____

_____   _____

Supervising Professor   Date

(Place the assessment packet in the department's designated place.)

Bibliography

Abraham, Neal B. "Facilities and Resources That Promote a Research-Supportive Curriculum." In *Developing and Sustaining a Research-Supportive Curriculum: A Compendium of Successful Practices*, edited by Kerry K. Karukstis and Timothy E. Elgren, 485–94. Washington, DC: Council on Undergraduate Research, 2007.

Adams, David E. "The Place of Undergraduate Research in the Teaching of Religion." *Journal of the National Association of Biblical Instructors* 3, no. 2 (1935): 88–90.

Adams, Liz, Mats Daniels, Annegret Goold, Orit Hazzan, Kathy Lynch, and Ian Newman. "Challenges in Teaching Capstone Courses." *SIGCSE Bulletin* 35 (2003): 220.

Agar, Michael. *Professional Stranger: An Informal Introduction to Ethnography.* 2nd ed. San Diego: Academic Press, 1996.

Ali, Farhan, Nafisa M. Jadavji, Willie Chuin Hong Ong, Kaushal Raj Pandey, Alexander Nikolich Patananan, Harsha Kiran Prabhala, and Christine Hong-Ting Yang. "Supporting Undergraduate Research." *Science* 317 (July 6, 2007): 42.

American Anthropological Association. "Statement on Ethnography and Institutional Review Boards." June 2004. http://www.aaanet.org/stmts/irb.htm (accessed March 21, 2011).

Angelo, Thomas A., ed. "Classroom Assessment and Research." Special issue, *New Directions for Teaching and Learning* 75 (1998).

———, ed. "Classroom Research: Early Lessons from Success." *New Directions for Teaching and Learning* 46 (1991).

Angelo, Thomas A., and K. Patricia Cross. *Classroom Assessment Techniques: A Handbook for College Teachers.* San Francisco: Jossey-Bass, 1993.

Association of American Colleges and Universities (Judith Ramalay, chair). *Greater Expectations: A New Vision for Learning as a Nation Goes to College, National Panel Report.* Washington, DC: Association of American Colleges and Universities, 2002.

———. *Liberal Education Outcomes: A Preliminary Report on Student Achievement in College.* Washington, DC: Association of American Colleges and Universities, 2005.

Astin, Alexander W. *What Matters in College?* San Francisco: Jossey-Bass, 1993.

Aubrey, Robert, and Paul M. Cohen. *Working Wisdom.* San Francisco: Jossey-Bass, 1995.

Bangura, Abdul Karim. "Metaphors of Expectations for Undergraduate Research: A Tale of Two Universities." Paper presented at the Annual Ann Ferrin Teaching Conference, Washington, DC, January 11, 2003.

Barton, Paul E., and Archie Lapointe. *Learning by Degrees: Indicators of Performance in Higher Education.* Princeton, NJ: Educational Testing Service, 1995.

Bauer, Karen W. "The Effect of Participation in Undergraduate Research on Critical Thinking and Reflective Judgment." AIR 2001 Annual Forum Paper. Paper presented at the Annual Meeting of the Association for Institutional Research, Long Beach, CA, June 3–6, 2001.

Bauer, Karen W., and Joan S. Bennett. "Alumni Perceptions Used to Assess Undergraduate Research Experience." *Journal of Higher Education* 74, no. 2 (March/April 2003): 210–31.

Baum, Joel A. C. *Blackwell's Companion to Organizations.* London: Blackwell Publishing Co., 2005.

Berheide, Catherine White. "Doing Less Work, Collecting Better Data: Using Capstone Courses to Assess Learning." *Peer Review* 9, no. 2 (Spring 2007): 27–30.

Biggs, John. *Teaching for Quality Learning at University: What the Student Does.* Bury St Edmonds, Suffolk: St Edmundsbury Press, 1999.

Bloom, Benjamin S., M. D. Englehart, E. J. Furst, W. H. Hill, and David Krathwohl, *Taxonomy of Educational Objectives: The Classification of Educational Goals.* New York: Longman and Green, 1956.

Booth, Wayne C., Gregory G. Colomb, and Joseph M. Williams. *The Craft of Research.* 2nd ed. Chicago: University of Chicago Press, 2003.

Bost, David. "Seven Obstacles to Undergraduate Research in the Humanities." *CUR Newsletter* 13 (1992): 35.

Boyd, Mary, and Jodi L. Wesemann, eds. *Broadening Participation in Undergraduate Research: Fostering Excellence and Enhancing the Impact.* Washington DC: Council on Undergraduate Research, 2009.

Boyer Commission on Educating Undergraduates in the Research University. *Reinventing Undergraduate Education: A Blueprint for America's Research Universities.* Stony Brook, NY: State University of New York, 1998.

———. *Reinventing Undergraduate Education: Three Years After the Boyer Report.* Stony Brook, NY: State University of New York, 2001.

Boyer, Ernest. *Scholarship Reconsidered: Priorities of the Professoriate.* Princeton, NJ: The Carnegie Foundation for the Advancement of Teaching, 1990.

——. *College: The Undergraduate Experience in America*. Princeton, NJ: The Carnegie Foundation for the Advancement of Teaching, 1987.

Brew, Angela. "Teaching and Research: New Relationships and Their Implications for Inquiry Based Teaching and Learning in Higher Education." *Higher Education Research and Development* 22, no. 1 (2003): 3–18.

Cannon, Katie Geneva. *Black Womanist Ethics*. Atlanta: Scholars Press, 1988.

Capps, Walter H. *Religious Studies: The Making of a Discipline*. Minneapolis: Fortress Press, 1995.

Carmin, Cheryl N. "Issues in Research on Mentoring: Definitional and Methodological." *International Journal of Mentoring* 2, no.2 (1988): 9–13.

Chapman, David W. "Undergraduate Research: Showcasing Young Scholars." *The Chronicle of Higher Education* 50, no. 3 (September 12, 2003): B5.

Crowe, Mary. "Creative Scholarship Through Undergraduate Research." *Peer Review* 8, no. 1 (Winter 2006): 16–18.

Csikzentmihalyi, Mihalyi. *Creativity: Flow and the Psychology of Discovery and Invention*. New York: Harper Collins, 1996.

Daloz, Laurent A. *Mentor: Guiding the Journey of Adult Learners*. San Francisco: Jossey-Bass, 1999.

Dart, Barry, and Gillian Boulton-Lewis. *Teaching and Learning in Higher Education*. Melbourne, Australia: Acer Press, 1998.

Davaney, Sheila Greeve. "Between Identity and Footnotes." In *Identity and the Politics of Scholarship in the Study of Religion*, edited by José Ignacio Cabezón and Sheila Greeve Davaney, 25–41. New York: Routledge, 1994.

Deal, Timothy K., and William E. Beal, *Theory for Religious Studies*. New York: Routledge, 2004.

DeVries, David N. "Undergraduate Research in the Humanities: An Oxymoron?" *CUR Quarterly* 21, no. 4 (June 2001): 153–55.

Doniger, Wendy. "From *The Implied Spider: Politics and Theology in Myth*." In *Theory and Method in the Study of Religion: A Selection of Critical Readings*, edited by Carl Olson, 193–201. Belmont, CA: Thompson Wadsworth, 2003.

Dotterer, Ronald L. "Student-Faculty Collaborations, Undergraduate Research, and Collaboration as an Administrative Model." *New Directions for Teaching and Learning* 90 (Summer 2002): 81–89.

Dykstra, Craig. "Reconceiving Practice." In *Shifting Boundaries: Contextual Approaches to the Structure of Theological Education*, edited by Barbara G. Wheeler and Edward Farley, 35–66. Louisville, KY: Westminster/John Knox Press, 1991.

Eddins, Nikolova, G. Stefka, and Douglas F. Williams. "Research-Based Learning for Undergraduates: A Model for Merger of Research and Undergraduate Education." *Journal on Excellence in College Teaching* 8, no. 3 (1997): 77–94.

Elgren, Tim, and Nancy Hensel, "Undergraduate Research Experiences: Synergies between Scholarship and Teaching." *Peer Review* 8, no. 1 (2006): 4–7.

Ellis, Arthur B. "Creating a Culture for Innovation." *The Chronicle of Higher Education* 52, no. 32 (April 14, 2006): B20.

Enerson, Diane M. "Mentoring as Metaphor: An Opportunity for Innovation and Renewal." *New Directions for Teaching and Learning* 85 (2001): 7–13.

Evanseck, Jeffrey D., Ellen S. Gawalt, Ayivi Huisso, Jeffrey D. Madura, Stacie S. Nunes, Remi R. Oki, David W. Seybert, and Ramaiyer Venkatraman. "Optimizing Research Productivity While Maintaining Educational Excellence: A Collaborative Model." In *Broadening Participation in Undergraduate Research: Fostering Excellence and Enhancing the Impact,* edited by Mary K. Boyd and Jodi L. Wesemann, 65–76. Washington DC: Council on Undergraduate Research, 2009.

Ewick, Patricia. "Integrating Feminist Epistemologies in Undergraduate Research Methods." *Gender & Society* 8, no. 1 (March 1994): 92.

Fink, L. Dee. *Creating Significant Learning Experiences: An Integrated Approach to Designing College Courses.* San Francisco: Jossey-Bass, 2003.

Foster, Charles R., Lisa Dahill, Larry Golemon, and Barbara Wang Tolentino. *Educating Clergy: Teaching Practices and Pastoral Imagination.* Jossey-Bass, 2005.

Foster, Nancy Fried, and Susan Gibbons. *Studying Students: The Undergraduate Research Project at the University of Rochester .* Chicago: Association of College and Research Libraries, 2007.

Foucault, Michel. *The History of Sexuality.* Vol. 3, *The Care of the Self.* Translated by Robert Hurley. New York: Vintage Books, 1998.

Freire, Paulo, and Ira Shore. *A Pedagogy for Liberation: Dialogues on Transforming Education.* Massachusetts: Bergin and Garrey, 1987.

Gentile, Lisa N., Nancy S. Mills, and Kerry K. Karukstis. "Faculty Mentoring Faculty: Lending Support Within the Undergraduate Research Community." *Journal of Chemical Education* 83, no. 11 (2006): 1584–86.

Gilbert, Lucia, Paige E. Schilt, and Sheldon Ekland-Olson. "Integrated Learning and Research Across Disciplinary Boundaries: Engaging Students." *Liberal Education* 91, no. 3 (2005): 44–49.

Gill, Sam. "The Academic Study of Religion." *Journal of the American Academy of Religion* 62, no. 4 (Winter 1994): 965–75.

Glew, Dennis. "Designing a Research-Driven History Program." In *Developing and Sustaining a Research-Supportive Curriculum: A Compendium of Successful Practices,* edited by Kerry K. Karukstis and Timothy E. Elgren, 388–89. Washington DC: Council on Undergraduate Research, 2007.

Gonzalez, Cristina. "Undergraduate Research, Graduate Mentoring, and the University's Mission." *Science* 293 (August 2001): 1624–26.

Goodall, H. L., Jr. *Writing the New Ethnography.* Walnut Creek, CA: AltaMira Press, 2000.

Grobman, Laurie. "Affirming the Independent Researcher Model: Undergraduate Research in the Humanities." *CUR Quarterly* (2007): 24.

Guillory, John. "The Ethical Practice of Modernity: The Example of Reading." In *The Turn to Ethics,* edited by Marjorie Garber, Beatrice Hanssen, and Rebecca L. Walkowitz, 29–46. New York: Routledge, 2000.

Guterman, Lila. "What Good Is Undergraduate Research, Anyway?" *The Chronicle of Higher Education* 53, no. 50 (August 17, 2007).

Hammerman, Susan Summerfield, Barbara Kern, Rebecca Starkey, and Anne Taylor. "College Students, Cookies and Collections: Using Holiday Study Breaks to

Encourage Undergraduate Research in Special Collections." *Collection Building* 25, no. 4 (Bradford: 2006): 145–55.

Hammick, Marilyn, and Sandra Acker. "Undergraduate Research Supervision: A Gender Analysis." *Studies in Higher Education* 23, no. 3 (October 1998): 335–48.

Hanson, Howard P. "Letter to the Editor: Student Research in All Disciplines." *The Chronicle of Higher Education* 52, Issue 40 (June 9, 2006): B17.

Harkness, S. Suzan J., Valbona Bejleri, Deepak Kumar, Ahmet Zeytinci, Rachel M. Petty, and Freddie M. Dixon "Integrating Undergraduate Research Activities into a Campus-Wide Initiative." In *Broadening Participation in Undergraduate Research: Fostering Excellence and Enhancing the Impact,* edited by Mary K. Boyd and Jodi L. Wesemann, 140–146. Washington DC: Council on Undergraduate Research, 2009.

Hathaway, Russell S., Biren A. Nagda, and Sandra Gregerman. "The Relationship of Undergraduate Research Participation to Graduate and Professional Education Pursuit: An Empirical Study." *Journal of College Student Development* 43, no. 5 (2002): 614–31.

Hattie, John, and H. W. Marsh, "The Relationship between Research and Teaching: A Meta-Analysis." *Review of Educational Research* 66, no. 4 (1996): 507–42.

Heck, Barbara, Elizabeth Preston, and Bill Svec. "A Survival Guide to Archival Research," http://www.historians.org/perspectives/issues/2004/0412/0412arc1.cfm (accessed March 15, 2011).

Herling, Bradley L. *A Beginner's Guide to the Study of Religion.* London: Continuum Books, 2007.

Heylings, D. J. A., and V. N. Tariq. "Reflection and Feedback on Learning: A Strategy for Undergraduate Research Project Work." *Assessment & Evaluation in Higher Education* 26, no. 2 (April 2001): 153–64.

Hill, Michael R. *Archival Strategies and Techniques.* Thousand Oaks, CA: SAGE Publications, Inc., 1993.

Hooks, Bell. *Teaching to Transgress: Education as the Practice of Freedom.* New York: Routledge, 1994.

Hu, Shouping, George D. Kuh, and Joy Gaston Gayles. "Engaging Undergraduate Students in Research Activities: Are Research Universities Doing a Better Job?" *Innovative Higher Education* 32, no. 3 (2007): 171.

Hu, Shouping, Kathyrine Scheuch, and Robert Schwartz, Joy Gaston Gayles, and Shaoqing Li. *Reinventing Undergraduate Education: Engaging College Students in Research and Creative Activities. ASHE Higher Education Report* 33, no. 4 (2008): 1–103.

Huang, Chungliang Al, and Jerry Lynch. *Mentoring: The Tao of Giving and Receiving.* San Francisco: HarperSanFrancisco, 1995.

Hunter, Philip. "Undergraduate Research. Winning the Battle for Students Hearts and Minds." *EMBO Reports* 8, no. 8 (2007): 717–719.

Ishiyama, John. "Does Early Participation in Undergraduate Research Benefit Social Science and Humanities Students?" *College Student Journal* 36, no. 3 (September 2002): 381–87.

Jacobi, Maryann. "Mentoring and Undergraduate Academic Success: A Literature Review." *Review of Educational Research* 61, no. 4 (Winter 1991): 505–32.

Jacobson, Robert L. "Professors Who Teach More Are Paid Less, Study Finds." *Chronicle of Higher Education* 38, no. 32 (April 15, 1992): 17.

Johnson, W. Brad. *On Being a Mentor: A Guide for Higher Education Faculty*. London: Routledge, 2007.

"Joint Statement of Principles in Support of Undergraduate Research, Scholarship, and Creative Activities." NCUR Board of Governors, April 2005, CUR Governing Board, June 2005. http://ncur.org/ugresearch.htm.

Jones, Janet L., and Marcie M. Draheim. "Mutual Benefits: Undergraduate Assistance in Faculty Scholarship." *Journal on Excellence in College Teaching* 5, no. 2 (1994): 85–96.

Karukstis, Kerry K., and Timothy E. Elgren, eds. *Developing and Sustaining a Research Supportive Curriculum: A Compendium of Successful Practices*. Washington, DC: Council on Undergraduate Research, 2007.

Katkin, Wendy. "The Boyer Commission Report and Its Impact on Undergraduate Research." In "Valuing and Supporting Undergraduate Research," edited by Joyce Kinkead. Special issue, *New Directions for Teaching and Learning* 93 (2003): 19–38.

Keasley, Alphonse, and Angela Johnson, "Linking into the Academic Network: Supporting Student Success and Program Growth." In *Developing and Sustaining a Research-Supportive Curriculum: A Compendium of Successful Practices*, edited by Kerry K. Karukstis and Timothy E. Elgren, 345–351. Washington DC: Council on Undergraduate Research, 2007.

Kinkead, Joyce. "Learning Through Inquiry: An Overview of Undergraduate Research." In "Valuing and Supporting Undergraduate Research," edited by Joyce Kinkead. Special issue, *New Directions for Teaching and Learning* 93 (2003): 5–17.

Klein, Julie Thompson. *Interdisciplinarity: History, Theory and Practice*. Detroit: Wayne State University Press, 1990.

Kram, Kathy E. "Phases of the Mentor Relationship." *Academy of Management Journal* 26, no. 4 (1983): 608–25.

Kunin, Seth D. *Theories of Religion: A Reader*. New Brunswick: Rutgers University Press, 2006.

Lanci, John R. "To Teach Without a Net." In *Walk in the Ways of Wisdom*, edited by Shelly Matthews et al., 58–73. New York: Trinity Press International, 2003.

Lancy, David F. "What One Faculty Member Does to Promote Undergraduate Research." In "Valuing and Supporting Undergraduate Research," edited by Joyce Kinkead. Special issue, *New Directions for Teaching and Learning* 93 (2003): 87–92.

Leckie, Gloria J. "Desperately Seeking Citations: Uncovering Faculty Assumptions about the Undergraduate Research Process," *Journal of Academic Librarianship* 22, no. 3 (May 1996): 201–5.

Leskes, Andrea, and Ross Miller. *Purposeful Pathways: Helping Students Achieve Key Learning Outcomes*. Washington, DC: Association of American Colleges and Universities, 2006.

Light, Richard. "The Harvard Assessment Seminars: Second Report." *Explorations with Students and Faculty about Teaching, Learning, and Student Life*. Cambridge, MA: Harvard University Graduate School of Educartion, 1992.

———. *Making the Most of College*. Cambridge: Harvard University Press, 2001.

Long, Charles H. "God-Talk with Black Thinkers," Drew University, September 27, 2008.

Lopatto, David. "The Essential Features of Undergraduate Research." *CUR Quarterly* 23, no. 3 (March 2003): 139–42.

———. "Undergraduate Research as a Catalyst for Liberal Learning." *Peer Review* 8, no. 1 (Winter 2006): 22–25.

MacGregor, Jean, "Collaborative Learning: Shared Inquiry as a Process of Reform." In "The Changing Face of College Teaching," edited by M. D. Svinicki. Special issue, *New Directions for Teaching and Learning* 42 (1990): 19–30.

Magolda, Marcia Baxter, and Patricia M. King, eds. *Learning Partnerships: Theory and Models of Practice to Educate for Self-Authorship*. Sterling, VA: Stylus, 2004.

Malachowski, Mitchell . "The Mentoring Role in Undergraduate Research Projects." *CUR Quarterly* 12, no. 4 (December 1996): 91–93, 105–6.

———. "Promoting Undergraduate Research in Non-Science Areas at Predominantly Undergraduate Institutions," *CUR Quarterly* 19, no. 3 (March 1999): 126–30.

———. "A Research-Across-the-Curriculum Movement," *New Directions for Teaching and Learning* 93 (2003): 55.

———. "Undergraduate Research as the Next Great Faculty Divide." *Peer Review* 17 (Winter 2006): 26–27.

McBurney, Donald H., and Theresa L. White. *Research Methods*, 7th ed. Belmont, CA: Wadsworth Publishing Company, 2007.

McDorman, Todd. "Promoting Undergraduate Research in the Humanities: Three Collaborative Approaches." *CUR Quarterly* 25, no. 1 (September 2004): 39–42.

Merkel, Carolyn Ash. "Undergraduate Research at the Research Universities." *New Directions for Teaching and Learning* 93 (2003): 48.

Middle States Commission on Higher Education. *Student Learning Assessment: Options and Resources*. Philadelphia: Middle States Commission on Higher Education, 2003.

Modiano, Raimonda, Leroy F. Searle, and Peter Shillingsburg, eds. *Voice, Text, Hypertext: Emerging Practices in Textual Studies*. Seattle: University of Washington Press, 2004.

Monte, Aaron. "Mentor Expectations and Student Responsibilities in Undergraduate Research." *CUR Quarterly* 22, no. 2 (2001): 66–71.

Moon, Dawne. *God, Sex and Politics: Homosexuality and Everyday Theologies*. Chicago: University of Chicago Press, 2004.

Mullen, Carol A. "Naturally Occurring Student-Faculty Mentoring Relationships: A Literature Review." In *The Blackwell Handbook of Mentoring: A Multiple Perspectives Approach*, edited by Tammy D. Allen and Lillian T. Eby, 119–38. Malden, MA: Blackwell, 2007.

Nagda, B. A. "Undergraduate Student-Faculty Research Partnerships Affect Student Retention." *Review of Higher Education* 22 (1998): 55–72.

National Conferences on Undergraduate Research and Council on Undergraduate
    Research. "Joint Statement of Principles in Support of Undergraduate Research,
    Scholarship, and Creative Activities." http://www.ncur.org/ugresearch.htm and
    http://www.cur.org/SummitPosition.html. (accessed August 23, 2007).

Nilson, Linda B. *Teaching at Its Best: A Research-Based Resource for College Instructors.*
    Bolton, MA: Anker Publishing Company, Inc., 1998.

Nnadozie, E, J. Ishiyama, and J. Chon. "Undergraduate Research Internships and
    Graduate School Success." *Journal of College Student Development* 42 (2001):
    145–56.

Olson, Carl. *Theory and Method in the Study of Religion: A Selection of Critical Readings.*
    Belmont, CA: Wadsworth, 2003.

O'Reilly, Karen. *Ethnographic Methods.* London: Routledge, 2005.

Otto, Mary L. "Mentoring: An Adult Developmental Perspective." *New Directions for
    Teaching and Learning* 57 (1994): 15–24.

Pals, Daniel L. *Eight Theories of Religion.* 2nd ed. New York: Oxford University Press,
    2006.

Parsloe, Eric, and Monika Wray. *Coaching and Mentoring: Practical Methods to Improve
    Learning.* London: Kogan Place, 2000.

Patterson, Barbara A. "Ethnography as Pedagogy: Learning and Teaching in a Religion
    Department Internship Class." *Teaching Theology and Religion* 6, no. 1 (2003): 24–34.

Perlman, Baron, and Lee I. McCann. "Undergraduate Research Experiences in
    Psychology: A National Study of Courses and Curricula." *Teaching of Psychology*
    32, no. 1 (2005): 5–14.

Reinarz, Alice G., and Eric R. White, eds. "Beyond Teaching to Mentoring." Special
    issue, *New Directions for Teaching and Learning* 85 (2001).

Reisberg, Leo. "Research by Undergraduates Proliferates but Is Some of It Just
    Glorified Homework?" *The Chronicle of Higher Education* 44, no. 37 (May 22,
    1998): A45–47.

Rice, R. Eugene. "The Academic Professional in Transition: Toward a New Social
    Fiction." *Teaching Sociology* 14 (1986): 12–23.

———. "Beyond *Scholarship Reconsidered*: Toward an Enlarged Vision of the Scholarly
    Work of Faculty Members." In "Scholarship in the Postmodern Era," edited by
    K. J. Zahorski. Special issue, *New Directions for Teaching and Learning* 90 (2002):
    7–17.

Rogers, V. Daniel, "Surviving the 'Culture Shock' of Undergraduate Research in the
    Humanities," *CUR Quarterly* 23, no. 1 (March 2003): 132–35.

Root-Bernstein, Robert, and Michele Root-Bernstein. *Sparks of Genius: The Thirteen
    Thinking Tools of the World's Most Creative People.* Boston: Houghton-Mifflin,
    1999.

Schantz, Mark S. "Undergraduate Research in the Humanities: Challenges and
    Prospects." *CUR Quarterly* 29, no. 2 (Winter 2008): 26–29.

Schilt, Paige, and Lucia Albino Gilbert. "Undergraduate Research in the Humanities:
    Transforming Expectations at a Research University." *CUR Quarterly* 28, no. 94
    (Summer 2008): 53.

Schüssler Fiorenza, Elisabeth. *Bread Not Stone: The Challenge of Feminist Biblical Interpretation.* Boston: Beacon Press, 1984.

Scisney-Matlock, Margaret, and John Matlock. "Promoting Understanding of Diversity Through Mentoring Undergraduate Students." *New Directions for Teaching and Learning* 85 (2001): 75–84.

Segovia, Fernando F. "And They Began to Speak in Other Tongues." In *Reading from This Place.* Vol. 1. *Social Location and Biblical Interpretation in the United States,* edited by Fernando F. Segovia and Mary Ann Tolbert, 1–32. Minneapolis: Fortress Press, 1995.

Seymour, Elaine, Anne-Barrie Hunter, Sandra L. Laursen, and Tracee Deantoni, "Establishing the Benefits of Research Experiences for Undergraduates in the Sciences." *Science Education* 88, no. 4 (2004): 493–534.

Shapiro, Nancy S., and Jodi H. Levine. *Creating Learning Communities: A Practical Guide to Winning Support, Organizing for Change, and Implementing Programs.* San Francisco: Jossey-Bass Publishers, 1999.

Shore, Wendelyn J., Teru Toyokawa, and Dana D. Anderson. "Context-Specific Effects on Reciprocity in Mentoring Relationships: Ethical Implications." *Mentoring & Tutoring: Partnership in Learning* 16, no. 1 (2008): 17–29.

Smith, Jonathan Z. "Religion and Religious Studies: No Difference at All," *Soundings* 71 (1988): 231–44.

Spickard, James V., J. Shawn Landres, and Meredith B. McGuire, eds. *Personal Knowledge and Beyond: Reshaping the Ethnography of Religion.* New York: NYU Press, 2002.

Spickard, Paul, Joanne Rondilla, and Debbie Hippolite Wright, *Pacific Diaspora: Island Peoples in the United States and Across the Pacific.* Honolulu, HI: University of Hawaii Press, 2002.

SRI International—Studies of UR. http://www.sri.com/policy/csted/reports/university (accessed August 23, 2007).

Stefani, L.A.J., and V.N. Tariq, D.J.A. Heylings, A.C. Butcher. "A Comparison of Tutor and Student Conceptions of Undergraduate Research Project Work." *Assessment and Evaluation in Higher Education* 22, no. 3 (September 1997): 271–89.

Stone, Marion E., and Glen Jacobs, eds. "Supplemental Instruction: New Visions for Empowering Student Learning." Special issue, *New Directions for Teaching and Learning* 106 (2006).

Suskie, Linda. *Assessing Student Learning: A Common Sense Guide.* Boston: Anker Publishing, 2004.

Taylor, Charles. *The Ethics of Authenticity.* Boston: Harvard University Press, 1992.

Teaching and Educational Development Institute—Teaching and Learning Support. "Developing Course Learning Goals and Graduate Attributes." http://tedi.uq.edu.au/teaching/assessment/learningGoals.html (accessed August 23, 2007).

Texas Tech University—Chemistry Department. "Program and Learning Outcomes and Assessments (2005–2006)." http://www2.tntech.edu/chemistry/laassess.html (accessed August 23, 2007).

Thomas, Elizabeth, and Diane Gillespie. "Weaving Together Undergraduate Research, Mentoring of Junior Faculty, and Assessment: The Case of an Interdisciplinary Program." *Innovative Higher Education* 33, no. 1 (2008): 36.

Turabian, Kate L. *A Manual for Writers of Research Papers, Theses, and Dissertations.* 7th ed. Revised by Wayne C. Booth, Gregory G. Colomb, and Joseph M. Williams. Chicago: University of Chicago Press, 2007.

University of Georgia. "CURO Center and Undergraduate Research Opportunities." http://www.uga.edu/honors/curo/about/index.html. (accessed August 31, 2009).

Ventresca, Marc J. and John W. Mohr, "Archival Research Methods" in Joel A. Baum, ed. *The Blackwell Companion to Organizations.* Oxford, UK: Blackwell Publishers Ltd., 2005.

Waite, Sue, and Bernie Davis. "Collaboration as a Catalyst for Critical Thinking in Undergraduate Research." *Journal of Further and Higher Education* 30, no. 4 (November 2006): 405–30.

Ware, Adam. *Speaking in Rhyme and Riddle: Hybridity in Billy Corgan's* Machina. MA Thesis, University of Georgia, Religion Department, 2007.

Wang, Rui. "An Annotated Bibliography." *Serials Review* 32, no. 4 (December 2006): 227–31.

Ward, Artemus. "Qualitative Research Methods" http://polisci.niu.edu/polisci/courses/fao7courses/545.htm (accessed March 9, 2011).

Wilshire, Bruce. "Professionalism as Purification Ritual: Alienation and Disintegration in the University." *Journal of Higher Education* 61, no. 3 (1990): 280–93.

Wilson, Reed. "Researching 'Undergraduate Research' in the Humanities." *Modern Language Studies* 33, nos. 1/2 (Spring 2003): 74–79.

Wright, Melanie J., and Justin Meggitt. "Interdisciplinarity in Learning and Teaching in Religious Studies." In *Interdisciplinary Learning and Teaching in Higher Education: Theory and Practice*, edited by Balasubramanyam Chandramohan and Stephen Fallows, 152–59. New York: Routledge, 2009.

Wunsch, Marie A. "Developing Mentoring Programs: Major Themes and Issues." *New Directions for Teaching and Learning* 57 (1994): 27–34.

———. "New Directions for Mentoring: An Organizational Development Perspective." *New Directions for Teaching and Learning* 57 (1994): 9–13.

Young, Sue F., and Robert J. Wilson. *Assessment and Learning: The ICE Approach.* Winnipeg, Canada: Portage and Main Press, 2000.

Zachary, Lois J. *The Mentor's Guide: Facilitating Effective Learning Relationships.* San Francisco: Jossey-Bass, 2000.

Index